I0830872

VISION OF THE NEW NIGERIA

Libertocracy

Yemi Obideyi

Lanret Solutions

Copyright © 2006, Revised Edition 2021 Obideyi Yemi

All rights reserved

The characters and events portrayed in this book are fictitious. Any similarity to real persons, living or dead, is coincidental and not intended by the author.

No part of this book may be reproduced, or stored in a retrieval system, or transmitted in any form or by any means, electronic, mechanical, photocopying, recording, or otherwise, without express written permission of the publisher.

ISBN: 9798453153688

Cover design by: Art Painter
Library of Congress Control Number: 2018675309
Printed in the United States of America

*This book is dedicated to The fear of God and those
who delight in being spent to uncover, uphold and
enthrone truth, righteousness and justice.*

CONTENTS

PREFACE

Maker of man, God, is pleased to bless him with different times and seasons. In a lifetime, exists moments to laugh or to weep; to plant and to harvest, to move fast and to slow down. Each moment contains a package with which to express a reaction; convey an action or capture an occurrence. In His incomparable and unsurpassable wisdom, the Creator also equips each man with potential to serve. Given graciously to man are abilities with which to serve generations. When this service is done according to the desire and dictate of the Creator, generations of men rejoice, the earth ripples in gladness; the grass, the trees, and the "waters" thump up in accolade for, all things come together to work well. A man in a white over-coat with stethoscope on his neck attending to, and prescribing drugs for patients, occupies a capacity. A woman seating behind a big, veneered table endorsing cheques and dictating which to be honoured and dishonoured in a banking hall equally occupies a capacity of service. None of the twosome described above is however, more significantly needful than the cleaner in the toilet of the banking hall, who ensures that visiting customers are not assailed by horrendous and offensive stench of old excreta. Various capacities are occupied by the trio to serve their generations in different important areas of need. As these capabilities vary, so do times and seasons oscillate. Then comes the questions: Why should someone else, by virtue of studying politics or enlisting with a political party, become the qualified person to discuss and decide on matters concerning toilet cleaning profession, farming, commerce, transport, healthcare or banking? Again, why should the affairs of the people in different occupational orbits of a society or nation be left in the hands or control of those who know little or nothing about the occupation or its practitioners. Better still, why should medical doctors or major-generals in the Army be defined and regarded as professionals while street cleaners, garment makers, factory workers, farmers, artisans (masons and carpenters) etc., are regarded as insignificant and so, downgraded in society? Again, numerous as they are among the citizenry, what place is given to commercial vehicle drivers in our national planning and decision making process? Are they factored in as strategic segment of economic growth plan? Dealers in farm produce; dealers in factory commodities, all of who number in tens of millions in Nigeria and other countries of the world are left to float as if they mean nothing to the system.

All shades of occupation are capacities within the national system and one is not a substitute to the other. As a leg cannot truly be a substitute for the nose so are most distinctive capacities. It is believed that this book or piece is inspired to correct age-long anomaly in constituting government and as such, it gives recognition to the principle of occupational representation. It believes that all legitimate occupations/ or professions can be properly grouped to serve as the ideal platforms for constituting representative government. That if indeed these principles are followed, political misalignment, professionals misadventure and pervasive apathy towards governance which often characterize political games, would be expunged from governmental system. Above all, that the contents of this piece are capable of creating both a tension free atmosphere for governance and room for aligning with the creators desire, this is why the concept is termed Libertocracy.

All readers and subscribers are therefore enjoined to embrace and stand fast in the liberty by which freedom has come to man and not allow selves to be entangled again with a yoke of bondage, which notoriously reduces the best of men to a beast of burden.Libertocracy is applicable and practicable in all nations and human formations, it is a universal concept and in line with the design of the creator.

CHAPTER 1

Libertocracy

One of the most popular definitions of democracy is "the government of the people, by the people and for the people". In other words, it is a system that vests overriding power on the generality of the populace. It presupposes a due recognition of the fundamental worth and dignity of each person; equality before the law; equality of individuals and enthronement of the will of the majority.
Since its advent in Athens, Greece in the 5th Century, democracy has faced a lot of challenges. These range from the pursuit of how to realise its core objective of enthroning the majority's interests in constituting government to the attainment of the real essence of governance. For these reasons, the form and practice of democratic government vary from nation to nation within and across continents. The gap, over the years, between the postulates and realities of democratic practice necessitated the birth of Libertocracy.

By definition, Libertocracy refers to a state of being free from the government directly or indirectly instituted by others and having a share in the government of the day through one's occupation. It is a democratic system or practice which allows people to be represented in government on the basis of their occupation or professions.

Since everyone cannot be involved directly in the acts of governance, representation is unavoidable. When the means of achieving representation in a democracy are based on conjectures, platitudes and hollow sphere as had been over the years, the objectives of majority rulership cannot but be misplaced. The vehicle for prosecuting democracy across nations often known as political party does not necessarily guarantee the majority's interest.

In one breath, only a few people determine the candidates to be voted for in an election because the platforms of political party are perennially susceptible to the manipulation of party henchmen who dictate the tune. They act as owners or controllers of the party through their choice candidates who often, are foisted on the general populace to vote for. Fundamentally, this trend of manipulation across democracies had become integral due to insensitivity on the part of the people. As widespread as political party system is among nations, it has no natural bearing with human society. There is no congenital link between political party system and the socio–economic need or daily activities of the people. To this end, it leaves the people and the system at large in the vast ocean of imagination and fantasy. Contrariwise, Libertocracy believes that democracy would become truly achievable if it is devoid of extraneous and nebulous creation as party system and re-orientated towards the actual needs of the people in the society.

It underscores the fact that people within a country are located or identifiable within professions and/or occupations, which exist naturally to serve the physical and socio economic needs of the society or measure its relevance to the state, continent, or the globe. Libertocracy reiterates that no matter how small a legitimate occupation may be, it is of greater relevance to a nation than an amorphous entity that thrives on deceit just to grab political power. Owing to its hollowness for instance, parties often railroad the people's mind into focussing on ephemeral attributes as against intrinsic qualities free of racial, ethnic or physical appeal.

Libertocracy posits that the people are better represented on the basis of their occupations to which they belong as against formation of political parties. This is so because by choice of occupation, the people are suitably dispersed into different spheres of need of the nation in order to meet their own individual needs. Additionally, occupational grouping serves as a more equipped habitation for decision making. It makes representation fluid, natural and tension – free.

Besides, Libertocracy does not leave out any minority group under the guise of opposition. It does not segregate people on the basis of colour or creed. It incorporates in government all sections that contribute to the wellbeing of the society. Formulating government on the platforms of legitimate occupations in a country removes exclusionism and engenders the attainment of the democratic principle of the majority participation in policy making.

Again, it recognizes that all legitimate occupations are important and vital to the progress of a nation, and as such one profession or class of professions should not be underrated or relegated in decision making process.

For example, as a Judge in his wig and gown sits attentively listening to the eloquent presentation of both plaintiff and defence counsels, he is of no more importance than the Chief Cleaner who scrubs the streets, and ensures the sewers are always hitch free, any hitch to the flow in waste conduit for instance, is capable of preventing court proceedings and cause outbreak of epidemics.

The essence of both the Judge and Chief Cleaner therefore is to ensure sanity prevails in the two different fields for the good of the system. Both must have the required competence and sense of duty to achieve this goal and as such, should be accorded same treatment or at least equal and balanced pedestal in decision making process. This is one critical element of social inequality in political arithmetic that various models of democratic practice across the globe had not been able to tackle over the years.

For democracy to be truly representative, it should take care of both the qualitative and quantitative framework of the society or nation. Failure in this regard may have been responsible for the high scale of distortion, contention and conflicts over the conduct and outcome of elections for democratic governance. Indeed, for a government to be truly democratic, its arms or composition should reflect both the qualitative and quantitative distribution of the society.

It is no less than a major defect in the morphology of democratic setting across nations that the judicial arm of government is allowed to be filled and operated by professionals in the field of law whereas the legislature is left aloof. Is the judiciary not going to feed on the product of the legislative arm? Is the latter less important than the former?

By format and functions, the legislature stands out as the most defining characteristics of a representative government. It is the organ that distinguishes democracy from a military regime or an authoritarian system. The core of people's interest and day to day participation in governance are embedded and most poignantly expressed via the assembly of law makers.

Law making is no less, an essential part of life for it is the bedrock of nationhood. It is the instrument from which the executive arm derives its power and so other organs of government. Where the law is defective in conception, composition and connotation or misleading in target and orientation, it cannot but produce lopsidedness, misgivings disequilibrium and disorientation. To this end, the process of law making requires a broad-based arrangement that would involve those directly engaged in the field for which the law is to be made and their counterparts at the receiving end. Why would teachers not be involved in making laws that would affect education or children of school age? How far can society go when we exclude architects, civil engineers, surveyors, masons, carpenters and co from issues that have to do with provision and regulation of housing needs of the people? What about laws for agriculture without involving farmers? Again, to what extent for instance, can an assembly of law makers task the Governor of a central bank or the finance minister when the members have no bankers, insurance practitioners, accountants, financial economists, stock brokers and investment analysts?

Since all laws have impact on or implications for one field or the other in the nation, Libertocracy believes that those in the segment of the economy or nation are better equipped to examine, propose or handle such laws or bills without manoeuvring.

Government is all about meeting the people's needs. To this end, Libertocracy posits that legislature should be organised along the lines of identifiable professions, which incidentally reflect the gamut of socio economic needs of the society. These needs range from health to security, education, power, finance, agriculture, communication, industry, housing, water, commerce, transport and industry.

Thus, in place of a House of assembly in a state comprising of representatives of ethnic groups, we would have representation of the areas of needs of the people. Instead of having tribal or ethnic identity as the basis of participation in government, the areas of need of the people take the centre stage. In Nigeria for example, a geo-political zone comprising of six states, would have a General Assembly made up of representatives or practitioners of farming or agriculture, housing construction, healthcare delivery, aviation, transportation, education, labour, finance, water resources, nutrition, petroleum, power supply, commerce, communication, information, environmental management, sports, security, social development, science and technology, solid minerals, tourism, works, justice and industry.

Each of the field of endeavour identified above becomes a Constituency or group from which membership of the General Assembly would be elected.

For example:

§ The Health sector or industry:

Would be peopled by representatives of those in health related occupations including:-

§ Hospitals and maternity centres

§ Pharmaceuticals

§ Medical laboratories

§ Medical equipment dealers

§ Drug manufacturing companies

§ Hospital equipment manufacturers

§ Para-medical outfits etc.

Depending on the size of population involved, each of the identified groups listed above could constitute a platform of representation in the Zonal Assembly .

For those in the practice of Education, the platforms of representation may be simply as follows:

§ Tertiary institutions' employees

§ Intermediate institutions (Post secondary school or institutes)

§ Secondary schools

§ Primary school workers

§ Publishers and Dealers in education materials

§ Authors, Researchers and freelance trainers

§ Manufacturers of educational materials.

Same principles would apply to all other legitimate occupations within the country or operators in every sector. In fact no one is left out including job seekers who are provided for in the Labour platforms or compartment. By this arrangement, composition of democratic government would have an alignment with the natural formatting of a nation according to people's choice or segment of relevance. This automatically eradicates artificial division, chauvinistic comparison and competition as well as manipulation or manoeuvrings through political parties. It frees the system from wholesale tension, political turbulence and unhealthy rivalry among ethnic or racial components.

Under this arrangement, national integration is guaranteed because each part, platform or segment has its own functional relevance in terms of tangible input, impact and complementarity.

It liberates the political space from grandiose deception and phantom promises which had come to be the lots of party – based representative governments in Africa and beyond. A clear direction is given to each candidate and their expertise properly channelled for effective result.

Professionals are saved the rigour of being subjected to despicable lobbying or bribing of politicians or political parties.

Libertocratic democracy gives room for fluid decision making process and generation of informed views and not arm-chair opinions, which at best, represent half-truths.

There is freedom to match the power of intellect with practical, relevant experience in decision making and the act of governance altogether.

CHAPTER 2

Libertocracy is a conceptual framework derived mainly from the word 'liberty' and the affix 'cracy'. Liberty or "liberto" here means to be 'free from the government orchestrated by others, organised and propelled by ulterior motives yet decorated as the people's best interest. It speaks of freedom from technical alienation in decision making particularly with respect to constituting   government. Whereas this alienation may be directly hurting to the general populace, it is usually carried out subtly and covertly via political devices and machination.

If the definition of democracy as the "government of the people, by the people and for the people" is anything to go by, it means true democracy is not just about casting vote at a general election. Mere participation of the people at the tail end of a chain of political exercises does not guarantee an effective democracy. In other words, if for instance the ground for the emergence of candidates for election is skewed in favour of certain category of people than others in a polity, it means the final outcome of the process might not be a true reflection of the majority's position.

To a keen observer of the political process therefore, what should be of utmost concern is the size or proportion of the population whose core interest is being served by the system. Put more succinctly, the method, means and requirements for prosecuting candidacy for democratic governance should pass the test of transparency, populism and fairness such that the interest of the greater proportion of the populace is accorded utmost consideration.

Besides, this liberty equally encompasses a rectification of the technical imbalance in the composition of the arms of government. If an arm of government like the judiciary is devoted or reserved for practitioners of one profession, it behoves on democracy to provide for other professions in the other arms of government.

The affix 'Cracy' on the other hand, denotes the institutionalisation of the practice of being perpetually free from direct or indirect alienation, political imbalance and social dissonance. Libertocracy therefore presupposes a union or re-union of man's choice coaches.

This involves the freedom to;
Choose a profession.
Be recognised and acknowledged in one's contribution to the profession.
To represent the profession at the top most level of decision making or government.
 Promote the portfolio of needs of the people to the forefront of consideration in constituting people - oriented government.

By instituting this practice, the people being represented would not be at a loss of what to expect from their representatives. Accurate evaluation of the candidates' performance can easily be undertaken and publicly manifest. Conversely, Libertocracy frees people and indeed the productive capacity of a nation from being represented [or misrepresented] by politicians or political party members who inadvertently do represent party's government and not professions.

(ii) THE PHILOSOPHY OF LIBERTOCRACY

Human societies or nations are made up of three categories of people. Be it agrarian, semi-mechanized or industrialised, every nation parades only three sets of people in its chain of livelihood. These three –the new born, the adults and the aged – occupy three significant positions around which the cycle of life of the nation revolves. In turn, the interplay of activities among these key positions or categories prompts an unending umbilical relation-ship between the polity and economy. In clear terms, the creation and distribution of socio – economic values across the populace underscore the import of governance, the institution democracy seeks to fine-tune, enhance, embellish and make most effective and efficient.

The three positions going by occupational cycle are – the Prepara-tory, Active and Over –the –limit groups.

Preparatory group
Those being prepared for participation in occupations or profes-sions.

Active group
Those actively involved in one or more occupations in the system.

Over the limit group
Those out of occupational life (retirees, pensioners and the un-employable).

THE PREPARATORY CATEGORY

Everyone passes through the preparatory group as a pupil, student, trainee or an apprentice. It is the take off point for each member of the nation in readiness to contribute to the sustenance of the society at large. It is also undertaken at different levels to become suitable for new roles or higher responsibilities. It is the replacement base of the system.

THE ACTIVE CATEGORY

The active group comprises of employers, employees, traders, volunteers, non-profit organizations, direct investors etc. It is the engine room of the socio-political system. Actual creation and distribution of wealth or socio-economic values on daily basis are undertaken by this group.

THE NON-ACTIVE CATEGORY

Over the limit group are aged people who have retired from active involvement in daily business dealings or employment and those mentally or physically incapacitated.

Beside making adequate provisions to represent the interests of the various categories of people listed above, Libertocracy avers that government will become truly representative if the mechanisms of recruiting its members are situated within the orbits of core activities of daily living.

It believes strongly that since needs are natural to man and industry is as old as man, it will only be logical and wholesome to weave the process of selecting decision makers

around the habitude already created by the interplay of needs and industry. A libertocratic government is therefore a government based on the occupational framework of the society. It articulates that all societies are naturally endowed with human and material resources. It recognises also that the discovery and utilization of these resources to meet needs naturally distribute members of the society into professions. This distribution offers a unique connectivity of interests and mutually interdependent relationship such that each member is predisposed to discharge the innate qualities of his person for the good or advancement of the society and mankind as a whole.

Nationhood, the bonding between the people and their nation, is easily achieved under productive interdependence. First, people are situated in occupations based on abilities and potentialities. This necessarily knocks off tribal sentiments as the primary basis of coming together. Since every nation has diverse ethnic composition, occupation provides a level playing field that dissolves primordial cleavages. People get into occupation primarily to meet their individual needs. To achieve this pursuit however depends on how well they can do to meet the needs of others outside of their own occupation or endeavour. Invariably, the interests of those in one profession are directly and indirectly connected to the interests of others within and beyond the nation.
Providing a climate conducive for harnessing the innate abilities of members of a nation and guiding the direction and use into which their products are deployed should therefore, in line with libertocratic principles, be one of the core concerns of any people oriented system of government.

The interplay of creative endowment and exercise of choice by members of the nation oils the connectivity of interest generated naturally within the orbits of occupations. Since one house of occupation needs the other to complete its objectives just as members of one profession are insufficient on their own, mutual interdependence becomes the hallmark of the system. This serves as a solid plank on which patriotism can rest without fail.

By all standard, political party system does not have an architecture with which to integrate society along the fountain of mutual inter-dependence as highlighted above.

To libertocratic government therefore, the primary constituency of members of the society should be their occupation. Where an adult is not yet employed or engaged in any occupation, he becomes member of a segment of the labour house where the following categories of members of the society are represented:
Association of Personnel Managers of all occupational groups
Labour union organisations (sectoral basis)
Employers of Labour Associations (sectoral basis)
Retirees and Pensioners (sectoral basis)
Association of Labour Recruitment Companies or Agencies
The unemployed, the handicapped or special people category

In line with the philosophy of Libertocracy,everyone is either a potential member of a profession or occupation, or a current member or an ex-member. Exception may hold only for those terminally ill or mentally deficient.

A citizen does not need to abandon his profession to find his feet in a political party hierarchy only to struggle again to become relevant in his primary profession after
leaving political appointment. A citizen remains in his profession all through and does not lose touch under Libertocracy.

Libertocracy shifts emphasis from ethnic bloc to occupational grouping and directs attention from "place of origin" to place of relevance or usefulness. It underscores the fact that being a natural member of a society, an individual is qualified to be useful to that society to the fullest of his capacity. It eliminates political jobbers and shakes off idle politicians who thrive, more often, on oratory prowess and long speeches.

(iii) UNDERLYING PRINCIPLES OF LIBERTOCRACY

Act of voting in an election is a miniature aspect of what liberty actually entails. A nation may have representative government with all levels of executive and legislative leadership being subjected to elections by the populace year in year out and yet the populace may be far from experiencing liberty. For example, when in a neighbourhood, every person has to be sensitively concerned about his or her security and always suspicious of the other, it means liberty has been tampered with. Liberty connotes freedom from fear and uncertainty. Fear is supposedly reserved for those who are outside of the garden, the garden of legitimacy that is the protection of the rule of law. When an individual or group falls short of the rule of law, invitation has been given to fear because the individual or group runs the risk of breaking the hedges of the garden.

However, when citizens legitimately committed to the rule of the law are assailed by fear, then something fundamental may have gone wrong with the system. Liberty is impaired, not restrained under such conditions.

When liberty is restrained or controlled, the individual is put under check for a time or purpose. It could be to allow for maturity or appropriateness in time or place but the truth is that liberty is granted or assured. It does exist but only silent.

On the other hand, liberty may not exist at all for the individual(s) or institutions perpetually. This may be total or partial in nature. Where it is partial, the victim(s) may not easily recognize it because the same denial is acceptable by others.

Erosion of social treasure like trust among citizens of a country for instance, is an indication that the society is one step below the plain of liberty. This, in this book, is termed "illiberty", meaning "absence of liberty". Physically though, the people may seemingly be free to move here and there, they are psychologically and mentally in chains and fetters. The reign of "illiberty" is probably worse than slavery because, its victims (who ordinarily suppose to oppose it) glowingly accept its shackles and defend it as the way of life. Also, they do drink its pollution and parade its toxins without any sense of concern about being freed from it.

Absence of liberty is bondage. Often, this results from ignorance on the part of the individuals or people concerned. It could also be that normative values of the society had institutionalised a means to which succeeding generations have been rigidly attached without checking from time to time the validity and reliability of such means.

In postulating its form of governmental structures, Libertocracy takes into consideration certain underlying principles. These are:

That needs (not wants) are natural to man.

That industry is a complementary endowment to man to create socio-economic values with which to meet the needs.

That industry or occupation serves as natural habitude for connectivity of interests

That mutual interdependence of occupations is the linchpin of human society.

That the core objectives and pivotal goals of (representative or people-oriented) government are generally the same or strikingly similar.

That God, the Creator, is interested in the affairs of man and that the best of a man is to align with His (Creator's) ultimate desire, and purpose.

(a) NEEDS ARE NATURAL

Irrespective of colour, creed or tongue, every man (and woman) is born with the necessity for certain (basic) needs. Be it physiological, social, or economic, these categories or classifications of needs are the same throughout the continents of the earth. Needs, basically, are universal to man and creation. The need to excrete, or pass out waste, to eat and digest what is eaten etc, are the same to all.

(b) INDUSTRY AS COMPLEMENTARY ENDOWMENT TO MAN

Man is made with industry and moulded in industry. As needs are diversified into physiological, social, economic and psychological so are industrial orbits where man functions daily. A closer look at man shows that inside of him are chains of industries. For example, the passage of food from the mouth through the oesophagus to the stomach (where breaking down into smaller particles take place, followed by conversion into glucose or other forms for absorption) into the lower parts of the alimentary canal including the separation and excretion of its waste, are clear completion of industrial processes.

Within a man therefore, are various industries. The characteristics of living things -movement, respiration, nutrition, irritability, growth, excretion, reproduction and death- function with industrial mechanisms precision. Movement, for instance by walking or swimming follows the same procedure like that of a vehicle or an aircraft.

Outside of the man also, is the social industry that moulds him according to its values and norms. Thus physiological endowments are tailored or directed to take after such things as taste, language, and education and all such things as are needed to function within the man's larger society or environment.

Like the physiological industries within man, the social industry has its entry and exit mechanisms, conversion and absorption compartments, and acceptance and refusal industrial arms etc.

At maturity, the man or woman now combines his/her social and physiological endowment to function within an industry of his choice or according to his ability. Same man also has the liberty to remain in the industry or occupation or acquire another profession or occupation entirely different from the previous one. That is why the best in a man is revealed in what he does or chooses to do. His ability or competence is judged through his involvement or functionality in one occupation or endeavour.

(c) NATURAL HABITUDE FOR CONNECTIVITY OF INTERESTS:

As the body frame of a man naturally houses the intestines, kidney, liver, lungs, the brain, arms, legs, abdomen, stomach, etcetera so does industry or occupation to human interests. Diverse interests of people in a nation are easily harmonised and also taken care of by an industry or occupation. As it is within a community so it works across continents.

A manufacturing company in Asia for instance can produce to suit the taste and interest of consumers in the United States, who in turn would desire the goods and use them without being forced. Meanwhile, those employed by the company have their multiple needs met and sense of fulfilment accomplished simultaneously.

As diverse and unique as the interests of people in a nation may be, they easily find reconciliation and sustained harmony in industries irrespective of the type of government in place. Industrial output permeates the walls of racial and ethnic segregation. It pierces the barricade of religion and connect peoples' interests together:

Again, let us imagine that within the body framework of a man, an organ decides to project itself in the forefront and compel all other parts to subscribe to it first so that it (the organ), can represent their views or champion their causes. How will it be if the legs for instance decide to represent or replace the kidney or the head trying to serve in the position of legs? He who created them knew better to have made the legs of a man two and the head one.

Contrariwise, it is a political party system that often creates distortion among these interests both within and outside the country. It swings the pendulum of interests beyond its natural oscillatory limit and hangs it one end. Same system attempts to balance this anathema, by creating an artificial pendulum and hangs it also at the other end. Sometimes political party system goes further to erect another "pendulum" in the middle. In most (if not all cases), party system silences the original (natural, God-given) pendulum and replaces it with pendants of various sizes and shapes. The result of this preposterous exercise, often, is stalemate, confusion, shapeless and formless coalition which in turn, breeds collision, animosity, acrimony and vendetta.

So, the real pendulum is one and naturally unseen, yet it reconciles diverse interests by its oscillatory power denominated in time and epoch. A political party is the artificial creation that seeks to compel all interests to subscribe to it. And that is why, often, it is all about making promises (in the name of party manifesto's) and at the end , give little or no reasons why the promises could not be fulfilled. A lot of times, political -party based governments engage themselves more with extraneous matters and still do labour hard, deploying instruments of the state, to convince the populace that those (extraneous) issues are the real substance.

At best, political party system represents an elaborate scheme of distraction to the cause of advancing human society. Politics is not a profession and as such, does not require a class of people as practitioners. It is supposedly about decision-making and all normal human beings are equipped to take decisions. This equipment (also called will) is naturally situated within occupational orbits where it is better trained, nourished, tasked and continually challenged. Occupation provides a direction that infuses naturally with the physiological industry within man thus propelling him towards unbuckling the innate qualities of his person.

This is why professions or occupation normally have something new, they break new frontiers but political parties usually play around the same things. They (political parties) do offer new faces from time to time to contest elections but no new idea. Same ideology, same old songs yet the world is not static (they say). In the real sense, a political party is an artificial amalgam of people with the purpose of grabbing political power. Needless it is, like the sun shining hard in the night.

(d) MUTUAL INTERDEPENDENCE OF OCCUPATIONS

As a man needs the collaboration or cooperation of another, so do occupations exist to complement one another. Libertocracy believes all human societies-be it agrarian or industrial- are naturally, wittingly or unwittingly organised along this line of mutual interdependence of occupations or professions. One is a complementary extension of the other. In other words, the effective running of one occupation paves way for another occupation or industry. For instance, the Judge or Law court may not be able to sit or have a session if the sewer is blocked or toilets are allowed to overflow for a while.

Above all, within a society, anyone not involved in an occupation or profession is directly or indirectly living on the effort or competence of an occupation(s). This principle also avers that a form of government composed along the recognition of mutual interdependence of professions would enhance greater participation of members of the society in governance. Besides, it would provide a level playing field for balanced opinions and mutual checks among arms of government on one hand and occupational orbits on the other.
It will also facilitate collaborative efforts through which individual (s) not willing to participate in any legitimate occupation can be fished out easily. His pedigree can be unearthed without much fuss.

(e) CORE OBJECTIVES AND ESSENCE OF GOVERNMENT ARE THE SAME

Maintenance of order and achievement of Progress constitute the core essential of government. As it is with a man so is it with human society. Order, to the body system of a man, presupposes that each physiological compartment (or industry) within a man's body is at peace with the other and that, one section or segment does not fail in its functional relevance to the other(s).

Absence of any breakdown or disharmony within the body structures or better still, proactive resolution of such disharmony or restoration of such breakdown reflects the level of orderliness in the physiological system.

Again, readiness of the physiological system or government to prevent incidence of breakdown or dysfunctionality within the body, serves to measure the level to which Order is maintained or aided. Preventing a breakdown can occur through release of antibodies; enhancement of the immune system; avoidance of unhygienic water, food and environment.

Progress on the other hand, constitutes absorption and utilisation of the products of each physiological component or industry for the overall growth, and advancement of the man on one hand, and fulfilment of his desire(s) on the other. Primarily, progress centres on creation and distribution of socio-economic values and advancement of human society as a whole.

By natural coincidence, these core objectives or goals of the. Physiological industries (within a man) also define the real essence of any government especially people oriented government.

What differs from one human society to the other with respect to government, is mainly, the means by which these core objectives could be achieved. A parliamentary or unitary system of government (as we have in most parts of Europe) is to serve essentially same purposes for its people or citizens as the presidential system. Thus manifesto(es) or political party ideology merely exists to specify this means.

And as avoidable as they are, most of these manifestos are articulated to pitch political parties at the extremes. They do this, for two main reasons: First, the crave for identity and ; secondly to foist an ambience of relevance. In libertocratic government, professionals do not need to strive among themselves because each arm like a physiological component has its own relevance clearly distinctive from the other. Again, significance of each industry is denominated in its palpable functionality to the corporate system.

(f) ALIGNMENT WITH THE CREATOR'S PURPOSE

Surely, it cannot be faulted that man did not create himself. The more man strives to upturn the purpose of creation, the more he engages himself in the bondage of ignorance.

A reprobate mind does not advance human society but debases it. The best of man therefore, is to seek to align his own abilities and endowment with the purpose of creation only then harmony of knowledge with freedom produces liberty.

(iv.) DEFINING RELATED CONCEPTS

Being practical-oriented in approach, Libertocracy shall define industry and occupation in their real sense of application as follows:

Industry refers to a combination of efforts to achieve a wholesome; a process of integrating various mechanisms to evolve a new form. It can also be defined as a systematic network of efforts that helps to change a thing into another form or improve its state.

By these definitions, the process of an eye sending information to the brain about view, and the brain returning interpretation of the image or instructing the eye what to do thus constitute an industrial process, mental reasoning is also qualified to be an industrial process.

In a nutshell, there are three major types of industries. These are physiological industries, sociological industries and conventional industries.

(a) PHYSIOLOGICAL INDUSTRIES

These are the industries located within the body system of every man and woman. These industries process what man takes in and convert them into other forms for the use or safety of the body. They are naturally endowed to suit the functional characteristics of a living man, thus we have industries for movement, respiration, nutrition, irritability (escape from danger), growth, excretion, reproduction and cessation of all these constitute death. Partial cessation is partial death or poor health.

(b.) SOCIOLOGICAL INDUSTRIES

Preparation of individuals for integration into the societal framework of daily living takes place in the sociological industries.

Beginning with the birth into family, a child is naturally a member of this social industry arm. Teaching of social values, norms, identification and sharpening of natural capabilities, behavioural traits etcetera are core functions of the sociological industries. Thus education or schools (formal and informal), peer groups, associations, clubs, moral institutions like churches are some of the orbits where sociological industrial processes do take place.

(c.) CONVENTIONAL INDUSTRIES

These are institutions or companies created to produce goods and services (socio-economic values) for the use of man and society. It ranges from sole proprietorship to multi-national conglomerates. It also involves national sub-regional, multi lateral organization's set up to function along one area of human need or the other. Conventional industries are diverse in nature but unified in purpose. Be it in manufacturing, marketing, promotion, distribution or services, one is necessarily in mutual dependence on the other.

Though a manufacturing giant is a whole institution on its own, its daily activity is not complete if its products are not distributed to the consumer through the retailers.

The process of achieving industrial output leads to occupation. Thus everyone engaged in artisan-ship, apprenticeship, commercial services, production, etcetera is in effect in one occupation or the other. In this piece therefore, the concepts: Occupation, profession and industry are used interchangeably.

CHAPTER 3

Libertocratic Power Structure

1.) CHECKS AND BALANCES UNDER LIBERTOCRACY

A keen observation of the practice of various forms of government shows that power distribution is not balanced. Libertocracy believes that it is important for power to be fairly balanced among the arms of government before checking of abuse can be effectively achieved.

Power, being right, control or exercise of authority is usually graduated even in all political systems. To this end, power and indeed political power structure thus have substratum (substrata). Where the substrata are imbalanced, the pinnacle cannot but be lopsided.

In both federalism and unitary system or authoritarian and representative government, the ministries (which represent the fingers of the executive arm of government) are peopled by professionals recruited or appointed to handle issues within the sphere of the ministries. Health ministry for instance, attracts those trained and certified in health related fields. The same goes for Education, Works, Aviation, Science and Technology etcetera.

At the other end of the pendulum, is the judicial arm of government which is peopled by professionals in the field of administration or dispensation of justice. All principal officers and agents of this arm of government are legal luminaries or those whose occupations are directly related to the practice of law.

It would only amount to a caricature or travesty of judicial system if the chief justice of a federation has to be a member of a political party to be appointed into the position.

Or that lawyers and court registrars have to be members of the ruling party to function in law courts. If it is improper for the Chief Justice and other Judges in a federation to be members of the ruling political party, why then should it be for legislators and even the executive (president and ministers). If Judges are not selected on the platform of political party membership for the simple reason that they should not be biased or lopsided in the discharge of their duties, then it is both retrogressive and nescient to allow or compel other arms of government to go otherwise.

In the first place, it shows there is an imbalance in the substratum of each of the arms of government. Such imbalance usually bereaves the legislature of intellectual power and expertise in technical issues.

More often than not, this deficiency leaves the law making arm incapacitated and renders it impotent. In fact it becomes merely a rubber-stamping or arm of government.

Secondly, this fundamental loophole automatically relegates other professions or occupations to the role of second fiddle. The

Judiciary is a profession and it is important like any other profession or occupations including the sewage or environmental maintenance professionals.

This is why a country of monumental status like Britain could get into the war in Iraq only to discover, after 12 months, that she was misinformed in the first place about the purpose for which the war was prosecuted. The United States under George Bush (Jnr.) had claimed that Iraq, under Saddam Hussain had a stockpile of weapons of mass destruction and for this, war was declared against Iraq. Britain teamed up with her ally, the US to decimate Iraq and after overrunning the country, they found no weapon of mass destruction after all. But the question (s) can be asked: Did the House of Commons or House of Lords ask for the proofs of deposit of the weapons of mass destruction in Iraq?, if it did, were the proofs viewed or reviewed by the House(s)? If it or they did, did the House (s) understand the proof or evidence in the actual sense? Getting into the war of that magnitude on such a falsity is symptomatic of puerility of professionalism in decision-making. Can we quantify the losses humanity has incurred as a result of this type of mis-match?

In Libertocracy, professionals are allowed the opportunity to participate fully in decision making process. A profession reflects an area of need of the populace, so Libertocratic legislature represents all the areas of need of the nation.

For organs of government to be able to check one another efficiently, they should necessarily be at equipoise. Each arm should stand erect and present views from the standpoint of informed intelligence not rhetoric or long speeches bereft of field experience or technical skills. It may well be said that the age long misnomer in composing governmental arms without recourse to all professions in a country has largely been responsible for the failure in the past. For, in one sense, government had been misled into governing people and numbers when it actually supposed to govern needs and the structures of meeting the needs.

Physiologically, the head as a part of the body does not govern the legs, hands, kidney, intestines and other parts in terms of their number or significance of quantity. Rather, it relates to, and direct things concerning them only on the basis of need and functionality to the body. By this, checks and balances are integral, assured, and self regulated.

At equipoise, the executive would respect the position of legislature because failure to do so would likely result in failed decision or none-event. Should that happen, the ground is thus prepared for the impeachment of the president or head of the executive arm responsible for such decisions.

Libertocracy gives room for inherent cautions or checks. The executives for instance would exercise power with caution because the legislature is not composed of members of his/her political party who usually harbour ideas in party caucus from where other members of the legislature are lobbied into submission. The legislature would no longer serve as a room for promoting sectarian or short-circuited party ideas, but a place for championing timeless ideas backed by informed principles and pragmatic reasoning. Each occupation or profession serves as a check naturally on the other in a mutually

interdependent relationship. Because all groups of professions are represented in a libertocratic parliament or congress or general assembly, an idea will be sieved, weighed, and properly diagnosed to determine its possible implications on other professions beforehand. Thus any bills passed into law in a libertocratic assembly would have been assessed by those on both sides of the divide.

With Libertocracy, political power is inherently dispersed and dis
centralised. It dampens the potential for abuse and curtails any
tendency for absolution. There is a direct contact between orbits
of the decision-making and that of concentration of daily activities in the nation. It becomes easier for one arm to correct or
check the other because 'partyism', which constitutes a political
veil, is removed.

CHAPTER 4

Political Party System Compared With LIBERTOCRACY
This comparison focuses on certain fundamental issues as a lot of differences between the two concepts or tools have already been treated under the preceding topics. Attention shall be on the six major areas which are: The host-stranger phenomenon; racial division versus integration; resource wastage versus conservation; alienation versus accommodation; natural incongruity factor; and enhancement of national development and effective governance.

(a) THE HOST-STRANGER PHENOMENON

Political party is a stranger to the central port of societal decision making process. Within the physiological structure of man where industrial activities do take place in various compartments- there is no room for extraneous creation like a political party. There is no artificial or unnatural organ that asserts itself to take decisions on behalf of all other parts of the body structure. Only for a sick or deformed body, a supporting or an external device is required. Therefore, the political party is not necessary except for a sick society or polity which also intends to remain on the sick bed. Likewise, in conventional industries or companies whether manufacturing, marketing, health care, advertising, or commerce, there is no such arm or organ as a political party in decision-making or administration. All decision making points are integral parts of the industry or company. Again, the family unit, educational institutions, or peer groups- all of which constitute the social (sociological) industries- do not hire politicians or create political party arm to take crucial decisions for the training or up-bringing of a child. It will be agreed that most important decisions with regard to character moulding of every person are taken within this sociological industries.

By all standard, political party system is a stranger to the Need - Industry Nexus, which is natural and universally homogeneous.

(b) RACIAL DIVISION VERSUS INTEGRATION

Political party system evokes racial or ethnic consciousness because it plays on emotion and physical appeal. Such factors as height, colour of skin, type of hair, shape of nose and eyes often constitute the basis of political party choices. Consequently, it strives hard to identify those who can appeal to the psyche of individual through oratory prowess or physique and then draws the populace to follow after these physical characteristics and inadvertently stimulates ethnic consideration. It naturally divides the country on ethnic lines (directly and indirectly, consciously and unconsciously) because its focus is not on core-activities that form the nation's daily being. Mother tongues may differ from place to place but the heart of all humans speaks the same language; colour may vary (outwardly), the inner colour and compositions of all humans are the same.

Because humans are made of one stock only animals are made after their kinds. It is therefore sub-human to champion the cause of ethnic consciousness especially at such a level of national decision making process. Government by professions is hinged on deeper considerations of ability or weakness, endowment and functionality such that racial or ethnic background does not have a means of breathing. It unites people and fosters inter-racial interests and purposefulness. Thus integrating diverse ethnic groups for the fact that professions or occupation are based on substance that has life in itself.

(c) RESOURCE WASTAGE VERSUS CONSERVATION

Political party system is resource gulping. It gives room for elaborate campaign by politicians expensive publicity and creation of false impression. The dangers of these practices are that party candidates are compelled to source for fund to prosecute electioneering candidature and in some cases, such people have had to receive donations from outside their countries.

In developing countries like Nigeria, it is mainly the moneybags and more often, those who had looted public treasury through bloated contracts find it convenient to stand for election on the platform of political parties. Political parties themselves often require all candidates to pay huge sum of money to be allowed to contest on their platforms. It is therefore a concomitant effect that political office holders under party system would seek to recover the funds invested in electioneering campaign upon assumptions of public office. If such candidates are sponsored by conventional industries member or companies, it follows that such sponsors would also have to be compensated through public contracts and other means possible. Worst of it all is that, this money gulping exercise usually "compel" politicians into having godfathers. In Nigeria, such godfathers do support the politicians through all kinds of means including: monetary donations, rigging of elections through intimidation of voters or other opponents; eliminating or incapacitating other contestants or opponent(s); securing the party's platform by crooked means etcetera. These godfathers in turn, rule or direct the affairs of government albeit behind the scene, whenever their candidates are declared winners of the elections. Indeed, under this type of practice, where really is government of the people? Empty barrels, it is said, do make the loudest noise. Government by professions or professionals does not require elaborate electioneering campaigns or lobbying. As would be clearly seen in the chapters on adaptation to the new Nigeria, Libertocracy is about needs and the candidates are to be elected or selected to administer substance not empty promises of manifestos. It involves talking less and doing more. Much of the talking comes through palpable result.

(d) ALIENATION VERSUS ACCOMMODATION

Governmental structure based on political party system alienates core-practitioners of professions and occupations. It is a common knowledge that political party membership is viewed as the domain or exclusive preserve of politicians and not active professionals like bankers, insurance practitioners, journalists and media practitioners. Teachers, those in Engineering practice, clergymen, aviation practitioners and so on do prefer in the main, to exercise civic right of voting than to be known as members of political organizations. Yet, winners of party based elections do take decisions that have far-reaching effects on all professions and occupations within the country. A few professionals who join political parties are classified by fellow professionals as politicians and as such treated with kid gloves. This is often so because professionalism "dies" within political party system. A professional submits all of his know-how to the party hierarchy and interest, thus he or she is mentally and technically castrated. Party machinery always reminds their (professionals) members in public office, that they hold the office on the party's ticket and platform and as such, only what the party wants is right. Government on the basis of professions accommodates people and integrates all within a nation into the system. It allows each part to maximize its potentials and places all occupations on same pedestal of national relevance. As a physiological make-up of a man reckons with every unit and aids functional relevance of one to the other is the government of professionals by professionals for upcoming professionals (potential professionals), out-going professionals (retirees and pensioners), dependants and all and sundry in the nation. In the real sense of it, political party system does not and cannot produce true representatives of the majority of the populace. It reserves the platform for contesting election for only the wealthy members of the populace because its requirements and workings can only be met through enormous financial resources. Since the majority of the populace do not always fall within the class affluent, it follows that political party merely conscripts the people into voting to support the interest of the few (affluent) foisted on the masses in the name of democratic governance. This is not a truly democratic practice but an "affluentic" democracy or governance.

(e) NATURE'S INCONGRUITY FACTOR

Core foundation of each type of industry is rooted in nature just as man himself. Physiological industries are naturally endowed and situated within man to carry out their functions accordingly. Sociological industries (whether crude or refined) are equally naturally inherent in and manifest with man. As a family socialized a child in pre-colonial Africa so were the families in ancient China, Australia, Greece and Roman Empire. And so it was in the middle and early ages. Conventional industries also have their raw material resources embedded in nature by providence. Gold, bitumen, crude oil, rubber, agricultural produce all of which often shape or direct the focus of each type of conventional industry are nature-endowed. They were not created by men but by God. Political parties have no traces to nature, suitable enough to make them relevant. All nations can do without political party system but no nation can survive without industry. Conver
In many countries like Nigeria political parties and their government had pauperized many and thrown up confusion, disillusionment, misalignment and disorientation of conventional industries and framework. The more political parties created the more the agitation for more and the more their internal conflict. And

the fewer, the higher the degree of dictatorship and mismanagement. Political party is nebulous in form and hollow in substance. It is an elaborate fiction created to deceive the populace.

(f) ENHANCING NATIONAL DEVELOPMENT AND EFFECTIVE GOVERNANCE

LIBERTOCRACY guarantees placement of government appointees in their field of endeavour or areas of competence. This is so because it is the government of professionals by professionals unlike political party-based democracy where membership of a party takes precedence over expertise and area of specialization. The legislature, in Libertocracy is peopled wholly by professionals and as such would endorse only nominees found capable and competent for specific portfolios. This would galvanize development across the nation, make oversight functions meaningful and impactful thus enhancing governance in general. Every arm of government would be totally professional and standardized, enthroning meritocracy which in turn, stimulates development.

ADAPTABILITY OF LIBERTOCRACY

The system of government by professionals is naturally suitable for all human societies. It is adaptable because its substance aligns government structures with physiological framework and sociological system. This alignment frees the nation from tension and political pulsation often created by political party electioneering processes. Libertocracy is flexible and elastic. Its principles can be integrated suitably in all types or mode of governance.

CHAPTER 5

Vision of the New Nigeria

I see a New Nigeria established upon the principles of Libertocracy, guided by the fear of God. It shall be anchored upon truth, fairness, justice and love. Its system of government shall be without falsehood, manipulation, deceit and fraud. From the North to South, her people shall be one in words, conduct and action.

The New Nigeria it shall be, not known for oppression, doublespeak, injustice, individualism, bribery and corruption. Her borders shall be free of ethnic division, competition and conflict.

Her resources shall serve not a few but all her citizens and her multitude shall be blessed by it in real terms. Her people shall not be scattered abroad scampering for livelihood, neither would they populate foreign prisons or the world's record of criminals. The New Nigeria shall become a home indeed for her citizens.

"May Your will O Lord God, our Creator be done in Nigeria".

By all considerations and from all indications, no prayer is more important or appropriate for Nigeria than this one above now and in future.

The will of God is usually a parcel that meets need. It satisfies need perfectly and accurately without adding sorrow, spot, wrinkle or blemish. And this is the uniqueness of the supremacy of God's will.

Remember, it is perfectly made to satisfy Need(s) not Want(s). When you attempt to satisfy want(s) with God's will, you begin to delve into manipulation, mal-adjustment, deceit and falsehood. And no matter the sum of money you decide to contribute to the construction of a mosque or church cathedral (and their affiliates) or to give to the Alfa, Imam or Pastors/Prophet/Reverend or beggars after manipulating God's will to your own selfish advantage, you would have only succeeded in increasing your degree of inanity.

This is because, a part is a significant portion of the whole and a whole is a reflection of the sum total of its parts. A nation of ten people among whom two are owners of a chain of luxury cars - Pajero, Lexus Jeep, Toyota Land Cruiser V-8 series, BMW 7 series, Peugeot 607; Mercedes Benz X - class etcetera - is at best, a poor nation for as long as the eight people in the population are in penury.

Vision of the New Nigeria centres on how to meet the need of the nation through a re-channelling of our (mainly) human resource capabilities; sifting of our mentalities; and re-directing our thought pattern, values and objectives.

In practical terms, Vision of the New Nigeria (VNN) captures the real issue bedevilling the Nigerian polity since independence and to which it clairvoyantly provides solution. A package of solution revealed in a rather unique system of government called Libertocracy.

STATING THE PROBLEMS

To say that the situation with governance in Nigeria is appalling is to be miserly with truth. Indeed, the troubles with governance in Nigeria are not only inherent but hydra-headed. A plunge into parliamentary system of government in the 60's (an inheritance from our colonial masters - Britain) could not tackle the Nigeria basic problems. Three or more attempts at the American Presidential form of government had brought us more woes. Shall we talk about Military intermittent incursions that held the country for over 25 years (altogether) and bruised our national psyche and fractured the seed of nationhood with corruption missile? It is said that the Nigerian situation is a tragedy.

Tragedy because its plethora of human and material resources are easily dwarfed by its mounting and daunting political leadership problems.

or election of rulers into various arms of government had become a recalcitrant challenge to various political actors and parties or political organisations.

Nomination of political appointees or rulers through political party bigwigs has left the nation with poor infrastructure, insensitive style of governance and disjointed policy action. God-father-ism in politics (one of the newest methods of ascending political office in Nigeria) has caused untold destruction of lives and properties in various states of the federation; fractionalised the populace into destructive opposition camps with attendant incidences of thuggery and wanton looting of the nation's treasury. Selection through political party chairmen and or endorsement by traditional rulers (Obas, Emirs, Obis etc.) had variously surfaced as other shades of god-father ism but all of which had taken the nation backwards through an institutionalised act of sacrificing merit for mediocrity and senseless and reckless depletion of the nation's resources.

This leadership selection process has made the Nigerian situation complex and indeed complicated. For one, there is sustained emission of dissonance of cultural ethos among the multiple ethnic groups in Nigeria

It has heightened political mis-alignment and professional mis-adventure. Political mis-alignment occurs when for example, an individual who lives most of his adulthood in Kano city for instance (where he is based) now joins a political party and contests to represent his town, Mbaise in Imo State, in the House of Representatives. Or a man based in Lagos with his family and business now winning election into the House of Assembly in Katsina to represent Malumfachi people simply because he hails from Malumfachi. Like the man from Mbaise, he can only succeed in filling the position for the time being, not to actually represent the people of Malumfachi because he does not feel what they feel. Misadventure on the other hand occurs in two forms. The first is when a professional occupies a position not relevant to his career or occupation directly but by virtues of his membership of a political party. This has the misfortune of impairing his professional experience just as it denies the populace the opportunity of moving forward or solving problems pro-actively. In like manner, a professional in the right field or portfolio but who has to siphon the fund of the public to the purse of his political party or god fathers has committed a sacrilege in addition to being in a misadventure.

As if all of the above not enough, the Nigerian situation has over the years been worsened by large scale dis-orientation, mis-perception and mutual distrust and suspicion which unfortunately, have come to be part of the nation's political system.

On their own, the political class and various governments had for decades, successfully failed to integrate the ethnic groups or grouping due to certain factors. First, the various governments of both military and civil regimes, have been based largely on ethnic considerations.

Also, these governments had served only to dress open wounds, assuage frayed nerves or calm rising tempers without getting to sort out their causes let alone dealing with the problems from their roots. Indeed, some of the past governments of Nigeria did attempt to proffer lasting solution but could not succeed, due in part to inherent contradiction in themselves and the pod that produced them. Let us examine this further:

THE MILITARY

The Nigerian military set-up is run largely on ethnic considerations. To move from the level of a Colonel or Brigadier-General for instance, your ethnic back-ground or state of origin becomes a crucial factor. All those to be promoted will be selected on state of origin basis or geo-political zone. The men in uniform were already (and always) nurtured in ethnic consciousness and considerations before mounting political positions and so, such people could not integrate the various ethnic groups they represent(ed) because they don't represent the nation in the real sense but the ethnic groups. The danger here again (unknown to them and many of us) is that there is no end to ethnocentrism. In the long run, ethnic consciousness often ebbs from national level to the clan then to the family unit and further to the threshold of the individual or his household yet does not end there. Let us give an illustration here. Say Abu is a colonel in the Nigerian Army. And in line with the practice, he is to be promoted to Brigadier-General or Major-General like others on the basis of the state he represents. Thus Col. Abu becomes a Major-General from Ondo State (his state of origin). Then in government (Military Administrator) a new hospital project is zoned to Ondo state, Abu then fights to ensure it is located in Ode-Aye, a town in Okitipupa Local Government Area of Ondo State where he hails from. Now, Abu's promotion is no longer used to the benefit of the state as a whole but his home town in Ode-Aye, after citing the hospital in Ode-Aye, he goes to ensure his relations and "people" are employed. In turn, these Abu's people would view or perceive the hospital as their own largesse from the federal purse thus undermining discipline and uprightness or administrative propriety altogether. In some cases, the contractors to the project would not even complete the job because the whole thing is seen "as our own share".

And do not forget that the whole matter began with the enlisting and promoting Abu on ethnic or state of origin basis.

THE CIVILIAN
Civilian administration on the basis of political party cannot integrate ethnic groups into the grid of nationhood in Nigeria. Reasons are not far fetched. Political party zoning system for appointment is anchored on tribe or ethnic group or location. Check out the Obasanjo administration till date, you will see that each of the 36 states has one or two ministers at the federal level. The senate is made up of three candidates or senators from each state of the federation. The House of Representative(s) from each local government area of the federation. Parastatals, ambassadorial appointments and extra-ministerial portfolios arc all based primarily on ethnic consciousness or balancing and secondarily on, professionalism or experience. Yet, there is unending clamour by the ethnic groups for the position of the president. The South South has spent and still spending millions of naira in this campaign. The North East is not resting its oars and so are the South East, North Central, North West and South West. The question however is: have the various positions already occupied on the basis of ethnic zoning or tribal consideration produced the result for Nigeria or the ethnic groups?. Of course the answer is 'no'. Shall we then continue to wallow in the same political parody or self delusion?

CHAPTER 6

Application of Libertocracy in Nigeria

This system of government is not copied from any country or nation but inspired to solve difficulties associated with governance in Nigeria in particular and human societies in general.

Below is a hypothetical or practical guide for instituting LIBERTOCRACY:

IDENTIFICATION OF OCCUPATIONS OR PROFESSIONS

To constitute the legislative arm of government, all professions or legitimate occupations in Nigeria are identifiably grouped under 28 (twenty-eight) Houses. For other countries, it may be more or less. These Houses are named after the areas of need of the populace which are synonymous with the Federal Ministries in the public sector. By implication therefore, all private sector operators are eligible members of one House of Profession or the other as can be seen below:

LIST OF RECOMMENDED HOUSES OF PROFESSIONS OR CONSTITUENCIES.

1. Agriculture and Raw Materials Constituency

2. Aviation Constituency

3. Commerce Constituency

4. Communication Constituency

5. Defence Constituency

6. Education Assembly/Constituency

7. Engineering Technology Constituency

8. Environment Constituency

9. Finance Constituency

10. Health Constituency

11. Information Constituency

12. Industries Constituency

13. Justice Constituency

14. Labour and Productivity Constituency

15. Land and Housing Constituency

16. Nutrition and Food Substances Constituency

17. Petroleum and Allied Products

18. Police Affairs and Civil Service Constituency

19. Power and Steel Constituency

20. Science Assembly/ Constituency

21. Social Development Constituency

22. Solid Minerals Resources Constituency

23. Sports Constituency

24. Tourism and Culture Constituency

25. Transport (Land) Constituency

26. Transport (Sea) Constituency

27. Water Resources Constituency

28. Works Constituency

On the basis of the House of Professions listed above, General Assembly would be formed in each geo-political zone of the federation (South East, South South, North East, North Central, North West and South West). Into these General Assemblies, representatives of each group of professions would be elected by all members of the professions and in turn the representatives would elect the National Assembly members from the Zonal Houses.

Below are the specific grouping of professions and their constituent members:

PROFESSIONALS REPRESENTATION CATALOGUE
Grouping of legitimate occupations in Nigeria (including the unemployed).

PROPOSED:

HOUSE OF PROFESSION OR OCCUPATION
CONSTITUENT MEMBERS

1. Agriculture and Raw
   materials
Poultry farmers
Export Crops and raw materials
Fishery, piggery et al
Domestic cropping group
Agric equipment dealers and repairers
Agric input and chemicals' manufacturers and
   dealers
Raw materials processors (semi)

2. Aviation

Aviation engineering companies
Airline operators association
Regulatory agencies association

Trainers and maintenance operators
Crew members association
Space engineering and information technological companies association.
Meteorology

3. Commerce
Mega market Association (unclassified goods)
Minor markets associations
Supermarkets associations
Distributors & warehouse owners association
Consumer association
Re-cycled goods markets (unclassified)
Raw materials

4. Communication

Courier companies
Telephone companies
        -Landlines operators
        -Mobile
Information technology companies
Manufactures of communication gadgets and equipments.
Dealers in all communication equipments.
Communication services operators
Manufactures of communication inputs.

5. Defence
Retired armed forces personnel
Dealers in military hardware
Manufacturers of armoury etc.

6. Education
Tertiary institutions
Intermediate institutions - post secondary school, colleges etc.
Secondary schools
Publishers & Dealers in Educational materials

Authors & Researchers
Manufactures of Educational Materials.

7. Engineering Technology
Engineering Technology companies
Automobile manufacturers
Electronic manufacturers
Foundry engineering companies
Weighing and measurement companies
Electrical engineering
Mechanical engineering
Structural engineering
Mechanic and auto repairing companies
Panel beaters association
Fire fighters etc.

8. Environment
Waste collectors association
Waste sorting companies
Waste recycling companies
Manufacturers of waste recycling machines and special equipment.

Environmental pollution scientists.

9. Finance
Banks
Insurance
Stock brokers, company registrars and issuing houses.
Discount houses, bureaux de change and, asset managers.
Mortgage financing companies

10. Health
Hospitals and Maternity centres
Pharmaceutical and medicine stores
Drug manufacturing companies
Healthcare manufacturers
Medical laboratory equipment dealers

Medical equipment manufacturer
Unorthodox medical practitioners.

11. Industries
- To be divided between eight and ten groups as follows:
a. Personal utilities products (large scale)
* Soap manufacturers
* Cream manufacturers (body & hair cream)
* Body & hair products including soothing items
* Toothpaste, brushes
* Baby items including toys

b. Garment
    * Textile manufacturers
    * Fabrics and leathers
    * Shoes manufacturers
    * Cotton & wool industries
    * Manufacturers of textile related machines
      and equipment
    * Major dealers in textile materials, fabrics,
      Cottons and their equipments.

c. Domestic wares:
* Aluminium manufacturers
* Glasses manufacturers
* Lamps and electrical fittings'
  Manufacturers
* Beddings & curtain accessories
  manufacturer
* Dealers in domestic wares.

d. Industrial and general utilities:
* Packaging manufacturing companies
* Wrappers, sachets & pad makers
* Saw milling

* Wood chopping & allied industries
* Furniture & foam makers
* Manufacturers of packaging equipment
* Dealers in the above listed items

e. Vehicle Accessories:
    * Tyres
    * Fire Extinguishers makers
    * Jack manufacturers etc
f. Small Scale Industries Segment:
i.   Agro-Allied sub sector
ii. Garment: Designers, Tailoring
iii. Personal utility services -
    * Barbing centres
    * Beauty salons
    * Photographers
    * Mobile toilet companies
    * Laundry companies
    * Cleaners and washer men

12. Justice
* Grouping of chambers and legal practitioners according to the new spectrum of specialization of the court System. By this, all chambers be merged into seven main classes as follows:

i. Economic Sabotage Matters
 Chambers: Those concentrating on-
  * Corporate Affairs commission
    issues like company registration,
    representation, shares allotment
    and ownership matters.
 * State revenue matters
 * Financial practice and commerce
 * Public asset
 * Financial fraud

ii. Public Interest Matters Chambers
 * Offence under metropolis such as traffic offences, noise pollution, illegal closure and occupation of streets etc.
 * Issues under Internal affairs.
 * State Affairs Matters.

iii. Healthcare Matters
* Hospital Management
* Drugs importation and sales
* Fake drugs
* Patent Matters
* Drug Manufacturing and specification
* Medical Professionals misconduct
* Environmental Hazards

iv. Matters of personal interest
* Educational issues
* Copyright and invention
* Labour
* Rent and property
* Religion
* Human rights

v. Constitutional Interest Matters
* Issues on limitations of arms or organ of government
* Electioneering matters
* Membership of Profession
* External affairs
* Membership of foreign international

vi Special interest matters

* Special court
* Export matters
* Marriage
* Agriculture

vii. Others.

13. Labour and productivity
* association of personnel manager according to industrial unions grouping
 * Industrials union representatives
 * Employers Associations Representatives according to industrial union groupings
 * The unemployed representatives through the stop-gap commission (under
Ministry of Labour)
 * Special interest representatives- the physically handicapped (Eligible for employment)
 * Recruitment and personnel management
companies association.

14. Land and Housing
* Builders
* Bricklayers
* Carpenters
* Artisans
* Property developers and managers
* Land surveyors and draughts men
* Manufacturers of building materials e.g
  cement, asbestos zinc, nail
* Dealers in planks and building items

15. Nutrition and Food Substances
* Bakeries

* Fast food and catering outfits
* Drinks manufacturers-soft drinks,
  Juice and breweries
* Sea food et al
* Beverage and cereals manufacturers
* Manufacturers and dealers of
  Confectionaries
* Poultry and powdery food items eg.   Milk,
flour, cooking oil, pastries and nutritional substances.

16. Petroleum and petroleum products
* Licensed operators in the up-stream
  sector that is crude oil extraction and
  Production
* Petrochemical manufacturers and
  Refineries
* Dealers in all petroleum refined products
* Dealers in petrochemicals including poly
  Ethylene, lubricants etc.
* Oil servicing companies including rig
  and flow station construction companies,
  data analysis, safety consultants etc.

17. Police affairs and civil security Assembly
* Representation of police welfare groups
* Private security companies association
* Retired armed forces personnel
  Association
* Informant/public surveillance group
  including aboki, mai group and private
  security men
* Security equipment dealer

18. Power and steel

* Industrial power consumer association
* Domestic power consumers association
* Power maintenance companies
* Power equipment manufacturers and
  Dealers
* Power distribution companies
* Dealers in steel

19. Science
* Chemical and paint manufacturers
* Geologies and soil scientist
* physicists
* Public analysts
* Information technology
* Scientific equipment manufacturer

20. Rural and Urban Development
*Town planners
*Demographers
*etcetera.

21. Social development
* Old peoples home association
* Orphanage and widowhood association
* Association of non-government
  organisation including the red cross etc.
* Religious bodies or association including
  Churches, mosque
* Physically handicapped
* Rehabilitation group eg. Ex convicts,
  victims of natural disaster

22. Solid material
* Extraction/production companies
* Converters of solid minerals
* Distributors and dealers manufacturers
* Export operators

23. Sports
* Sporting associations eg. Football
  association i.e. Club owners athletic
  association etc.
* sporting equipment manufacturers
* Sport administration association
* Trainers association

24. Tourism and culture
* Hospitality companies tht is hotels, guest
* Tourism organizing companies
* Tourism centres management companies
* Arts and sculpture
* Musical associations
* Promoters, recording studio association
* Horticulture, artefacts

25. Transport (land)
* Intra-state transport operators
* Inter-state transport
* Dealers in mass transportation
* Manufacturers in mass or major
  transportation vehicles
* Rail operators and managements
* Commuters association

26. Transport (sea)
* Vessel owners association
* Shipping companies
* Boat transport operators
* Crude oil lifting operators
* Maritime operators association

27. water resources
* Plumbing
* Dredgers and boreholes sinkers
* Water treatment chemical manufacturer

* Manufacturers of plumbing materials,
  equipment etc.

28. Works
* Architectural companies
* Civil engineering
* Construction companies
* Structural engineering companies
* works construction equipment
  Manufacturers.

All professions or occupation serving to meet needs are therefore represented in the House of Legislature. As Medical Doctors, Pharmacists and Laboratory Technologists are represented in Health so are market women, palm oil sellers represented in the House of Commerce. Tailors, fashion designers and garment makers would find their place under the small scale segment of the House of Industries.

It follows therefore that there will be a General Assembly in each zone comprising of representatives of all professions in that geopolitical zone to effectively carry out legislative functions and guarantee even development of human and material resources. Each region would make laws within the region in line with the Federal Policies and Cardinal Principles.

CHAPTER 7

Legislative Chambers

These are the different levels at which major legislative matters do take place.

a) General Assembly
b) National Assembly or Grand Assembly of Nigerian Professionals

a) THE GENERAL ASSEMBLY

The General Assembly (G-A) exists in each zone of the federation. It comprises of representatives of each platform of professions in the geo-political zone.
The G-A is the only organ at the zone to make laws. This is because it has representatives that cut across the various professions. It also serves as a law-sourcing organ and zonal administration-monitoring medium.

G-A PRINCIPAL OFFICERS
To be elected by members.

FUNCTIONS AND POWERS OF THE GENERAL ASSEMBLY
To make subsidiary laws for the zone in such matters approved by the constitution or National Assembly which may include but not limited to the following areas:-
i. Environmental upkeep
ii. Housing: Planning, construction, rents, tenancy etc.
iii. Business Development including industry standards, rates, disciplinary measures, enlistment in industry or de-listing, co-operative efforts, awards, business associations, employment etc..
iv. Educational issues especially for primary, secondary and inter-mediate levels.
v. Market places - maintenance, new sites creation etc.
vi. Marriage matters.
vii. Welfare
viii. Religious matters
ix. Traffic control, safety standards etc.
x. Transportation
xi. Emergency control etc.

SUBSIDIARY LAWS:
In the main, G-A should seek to enhance the federal laws or provide details of how to make the constitution more relevant to daily developments within the region.
§ Any subsidiary law that contradicts the framework of the constitution or at loggerheads with federation principles may be nullified by the National Assembly or de-activated by .the Federal Ministries.
§ In any case, the Federal Constitution and Acts of the National Assembly are always superior to subsidiary laws.
§ Subsidiary laws are only applicable within the zone where it is made except adopted by another zone (s).
2. LAW-SOURCING FUNCTION
§ The General Assembly may propose bills or make drafts on crucial issues to the National Assembly for deliberation and possible

passage into law.

§ The G-A should make Subsidiary Laws to take care of the disabled persons in business enterprises, labour and educational training or apprenticeship.

3. ZONAL ACTIVITIES REVIEW

§ The General Assembly is to review from time to time (monthly and weekly) legislative and administrative activities in the zone.

§ It should point out shortcomings or inadequacies or areas of need with a view to upgrading the zone.

§ It should have power to summon a Task Minister and or any zonal official of a Ministry to explain issues before it.

§ Resolves conflict at all levels within the zone. It may have or initiate a joint committee (outside of the assembly) with or without the judiciary.

"Oversees matters of zonal mutual interest and review performance accordingly. For examples facilitating activation of new platforms in the zonal house.

Take complaints of the public (zonal) and impress it on the relevant arm of government in the zone. Investigate and deliberate on matters referred to it by the National Assembly (Grand Assembly Of Professionals) and make recommendation to the assembly directly on such matters, and to the Council of Ministers or Task Ministers on matters that concern them.

Review controversial court decisions especially, through its judicial committee arm and make recommendations to the relevant Joint House(S) and make Council of Ministers.

4. RESOURCE-EFFICIENCY FUNCTION

Set standards for the management of resources allocated to the zone such as refined petroleum products and ensure even or fair distribution across the zone.

Must maintain records of allocation and distribution of all items allocated to zones by the federal government including items like building materials for projects, vehicles for public use etcetera.

Visiting sites and ensuring timely completion of projects. Seeing to it that resources are not wasted within the zone but efficiently handled and managed for the public good.

The General Assembly is to be held responsible for any avoidable (loss) of resources suffered by the zone especially if it fails to take necessary steps before hand or immediately afterwards.

5. COLLECTIVE GENERAL ASSEMBLIES FUNCTIONS

The six General Assemblies are to participate collectively in nominating, screening and recommending only three candidates to the National Assembly for the position of the president whenever the National Assembly impeaches the incumbent or a situation of sudden death without the president nominating eligible successor beforehand.

COLLECTIVE GENERAL ASSEMBBLY FUNCTIONS:

JOINT GENERAL ASSEMBLY FORUM
 Members of the six General Assemblies (G-As) may come together to rub minds on legislative functions; share ideas and engage in personnel training.

It is not a legislative organ and therefore cannot make law.

JOINT GENERAL ASSEMBLY EXECUTIVE FORUM

As part of its oversight functions, this Joint Executive Forum should step in to resolve conflicts among the top echelon of government arms. That is whenever there is a prolonged friction between the executive and legislature (National Assembly) or between the National Assembly and the Judiciary (chief justice) the Joint General Assembly Executive Forum should take effective conflict resolution initiative and ensure that harmony is restored between or among the arms of government immediately. The forum can choose to invite eminent Nigerians or respected veterans to strengthen its team or effort.

This function of the Joint General Assembly Executives Forum should be reserved only for its top echelon and stated in the constitution as one of its extra-legislative and national functions.

LIMITATION OF THE GENERAL ASSEMBLY

Its leadership must resign or step down if the zonal Peoples Assembly should call for such in writing after a vote of its two-third majority accordingly. The people's Assembly Executives committee members must endorse this writing.

b) THE NATIONAL ASSEMBLY

The National Assembly is the highest Law-Making Body in the federation. It comprises of one representatives of professions from the six geo-political zones.

FUNCTIONS AND POWERS OF THE NATIONAL ASSEMBLY

1. To have superior and overriding power over legislative process or law making.

2. To discuss and legislate on all matters concerning the nation,

it's internal and external affairs.

3. Cancel or nullify any law or edict passed by the Zonal General Assemblies.

4. Can recommend to the president, individuals or Nigerians for ministerial appointments.

5. To also accept and screen nominations from the president or executive for ministerial positions, ambassadorial and any other.

6. To have overriding powers on legislations except when the President and Commander-in-Chief decides to veto a decision or on emergency situations.

7. Can summon a Minister to answer questions on national issues or issues of national interest within the minister's portfolio.

8. Can call the President to order on national issues or actions that are not in the best interest of the nation especially in the long run.

9. Can impeach the President by a vote of two-third majority but only on certain grounds for instance:

- Proofs of willful mismanagement of public funds.
- Consistent violations of cardinal principles of the constitution without consideration for the nation's interest.
- Sheer display of incompetence
- Impaired Health or conditions of incapability especially mentally.
- Embezzlement of public funds, ownership of foreign accounts, money-laundering etcetera.

10. Vetting and passing the National Budgetary proposals into law. This must however be done within a specified period say six weeks except the executive fails to provide information necessary for the passage of the bill. Such requests for information by the NASS should be made public.

LIMITATION OF THE NATIONAL ASSEMBLY

Cannot nominate to replace the President upon impeachment. Only the six General Assemblies should be empowered to nominate three presidential candidates from which the National Assembly should elect one.

CHAPTER 8

Electing and Selecting the President

PREAMBLES: One thing that should be pertinent to the success of the Vision of the New Nigeria (and indeed all human formations) is the factor of the fear of God Almighty.

In as much as Libertocratic governmental system predisposes governance towards fixing a round peg in a round hole; a square peg in a square hole; and achieving optimum utilisation of resources, its practice must be hinged upon the fear of God. It is the fear of God that regulates an individual from within, making him to shun illegality or evil even when there is no policeman around or a prying eye or the arm of the law.

Be that as it may, it is evidently clear that God Himself who sees the hearts of men is not a democrat. God does not make a choice on the strength of the number of people or size of population. If it were so, diminutive countries or entities like Rome, Greece, Persia etc., should not have ruled the world as they did in ancient history. What about Britain as small as it is had an empire, which extended from Europe to West and Southern Africa, Latin and Central America to the far Eastern world of Asia. God does not look at the size to make a choice. By simple observation also we can see that, the most populous countries in the world today, are not necessarily the most developed; the smallest nations too are not the most backward. Rather, efficient deployment of God given endowment or wisdom makes a whole lot of difference.

Democracy is said to be a game of numbers but above all democracies or democratic systems, God's order still supersedes. As beneficial as democratic principles are under party system, they do not represent ultimate creativity of God-given wisdom and solution, and as such, still leave a lot of challenges or Inconsistencies. Indeed, it has thrown up a lot of unanswered questions. For example: why is it that the best candidates do not usually win elections? Why is democracy always throwing up the same set of people around the corridors of power? Why should democracy in Nigeria and indeed Africa provide a comfortable platform for thugs and thuggery, street urchins and miscreants in pre and post election moments? Why is there always a general apathy towards election especially on political party basis? Why must democracy be so expensive or costly that candidates are compelled to source for huge funds to be able to stand for an election? How will a candidate who has committed so much money to win an election be truly fair with the public fund upon assumption of office?

Whereas the Vision of the New Nigeria places the responsibilities of electing the legislature on the people directly, it recommends two distinct methods for the election of the president. These are (1) Nomination through the General Assembly and (2) The two - in- one method.

(1) Nomination Through The General Assembly

Each General Assembly (G-A) in the geopolitical zone would nominate one candidate to the National Assembly. By implication, six candidates would emerge from six geo - political zones. The National Assembly would vote for the president to emerge.

(2) THE TWO - IN - ONE METHOD

The incumbent president would nominate one or two candidates or at most three to the National Assembly for consideration and voting. The candidates with highest vote count emerges as the president. If the incumbent chooses to nominate only one candidate, so be it as long as the nominee is upright, visionary and free of criminal record. Let him or her become the President.

REASONS FOR TWO - IN -ONE
An incumbent president is well positioned to see or notice the ability of his subjects including the citizenry. By right or law, he/she can access any arm of human endeavour within the country with or without notice, the incumbent can obtain report on any person or institution without delay.

So, only the incumbent understands what is required and only he (or through his aides) could fish out the right person. The eyes of every man are in the head. It is easier and better to see from above hence the Maker did not fix the eyes on the legs or elsewhere. Though the legs are more in number than the head in a body, the latter has sight to see and capacity to interpret whatever legs or hands may touch or feel.

Thirdly, since an incumbent is entrusted with appointing various officials into important executive or administrative positions such as heads of extra-ministerial organs all through his term of office, he is equipped and better informed to match attributes with performance or potentials with expected output.

Fourthly, this style of incumbent selecting his successor would prevent overt and covert campaigns by serving public officers thereby avoiding distractions and underground political maneuverings.

Fifthly, it prevents pretense and laxity in public office and public officials, and instead, stimulates commitment and productivity. It eradicates waste of resources, as anyone interested in the position of president would only need to work hard in his field of endeavour and not to engage in expensive publicity for that purpose. It is suitable for an environment like Nigeria where political structures are easily manipulated under the guise of holding a presidential or general election.

It promotes an atmosphere devoid of tension between the president and his deputy throughout their tenure.

Democracy does not always produce the best candidate or the one with the highest grade of merit for a position. This, in part, is due to the structures and workings of political party system which usually give room for certain considerations other than merit, and secondly a number of individuals are naturally averse to politicking as an act and partyism as a method even when they have the potentials or attributes to make the best candidate for public positions. On the other hand, most if not all constitutions empower the president or prime minister of a country to appoint individuals for strategic positions such as Governor of the Central Bank, Director-Generals for all commissions and extra-ministerial organs, ambassadors and special envoys to represent the nation. By dint of wisdom therefore, if a president can make good judgement in filling these all-important positions, why wouldn't he do same for the office of the president.
In particular, the system of professionals as detailed in this Vision makes it suitably appropriate for the incumbent to serve the interest of the nation in this respect.

RESTRAINTS ON TWO-IN-ONE

There should be certain constitutional restraints to guide against abuse of this method of selection of successor by the incumbent.

1. The vice president should not become president unless he/she is chosen by the third or fourth president. This is to ensure that a vice president does not take it for granted that he is automatically, a heir-apparent. Also, to forestall the possibility of covering up untoward activities or activity of successive governments over a long period, it is important that the tenure of a vice-president is totally tied to that of the president who appoints him or her.

2. A successor cannot come from the family, relations or possibly the cabinet (notably Federal Ministers) of an incumbent. A task minister is however not barred from being nominated for this position.
3. Should a successor be found incompetent through glaring evidences, he/she could be impeached via a vote of two third of the National Assembly.

Other conditions to be observed in nominating or selecting presidential candidate(s) are as follows:
- Nominees must not be:
 a. Principal officers of the Legislative, Executive or Judicial organs of government except from the level of Task ministers and below.
b. Must not belong to any secret or cultic group that promotes sectarian interests.
c. Must not belong (overtly or covertly) to ethnic-based association or group that seeks ethnic consciousness, nationalism or activism

THE CANDIDATE(S)

The incumbent to nominate or recommend one candidate or at most two to the National Assembly which in turn would endorse or elect (if nominees are more than one). If the candidate recommended by the president fulfils constitutional requirement as stated above, the National Assembly should not request for more nominees or attempt to judge by ethnic considerations,

THE PRESIDENT'S TERM OF OFFICE

(a) TERMS OF OFFICE: for developing or third world countries like Nigeria, that are in dire need of basic structures for development in all areas of endeavour, the constitution should allow for Nine (9) years tenure for the president per term. This is so because, for the structures to be erected, there is need for excavation, removal and clearing of age-long anti-social mentalities; retrogressive cultural beliefs and practices; unsavoury values and esteemed individualism.

Without a proper foundation of nationhood and social cohesion, development objectives cannot be realised in real terms let alone sustained or multiplied.

So, the nine-year tenure of the president should serve as full term but divided into two equal halves of four and half years as follows.

HALF-TERM STEWARDSHIP

At the end of the first half, the president should address the nation and in particular, render his/her stewardship to the nation and the National Assembly at the end of the last month of the fourth year.

At this forum, the National Assembly members may ask questions or seek clarifications on issues. Thereafter the Assembly would decide by vote or any method it chooses whether the president should continue the second half or discontinue. Approval of the National Assembly should be based on simple majority vote and must be conveyed statutorily through a letter to Mr. President.

2ND HALF TERM:-
Rendering of stewardship for the whole period of first and second halves should again be made by the president at the end of the six month of the ninth year, (that is six months to the end of the full term). After the question and answer session that follows, president physically would indicate his/her interest to continue or discontinue. If he or she chooses to continue, would then offer himself or herself for voting before the National Assembly. This would be only for the second term.

CHAPTER 9

The Executive

Government of professionals is a direct anti-dote to contract award cancer in Nigeria. The executive arm under this system of government does not award contract instead it employs full-fledged professionals, mobilize them adequately and deploys its human resource portfolio to execute projects from conception to commissioning. "No Contract Award-Principle" is an essential component of the Government of professionals.

The federal ministry here is not a civil service (for political apologists or contractors' messengers) but one to be proud of having mastery of its field with track record of notable projects directly handled by it; one with credentials of superlative performance strong enough to compete locally and internationally. British Petroleum and Statoil are arms of the British and Norwich Ministries of petroleum respectively and each of them had operated in the Nigerian oil sector with successful results.

Under the current arrangement (and as it has always been), the impact of each federal ministry including their potentiality to generate substantial income is lost because they all reside in fanciful buildings in Abuja and award projects (including conception of what to do) to contractors.

Each federal ministry should be headquartered in the six geo-political zones. Not to spend fortunes to construct their office complexes, no, not at all, construction companies which successive governments in Nigeria paid heavy sum of money only make use of portakabins and make-shift offices to get their job done. This is a lesson for us. Many of the construction giants have White people or Europeans and yet do make do with these make-shift offices to take away a lot of resources from Nigeria.

The ministry practically would have specific arms to handle: project designs, raw materials sourcing and processing and construction of projects. Contracts award should be allowed only on a areas where there are no Nigerian experts or recruitable personnel for the ministries concerned. (Please do note that it is for Needs not Wants)

For instance, the Ministry of Agriculture would have North West Farm, South East Farm, South South Farm and North East Farm each manned effectively by professionals whose work will be measured daily by practical or tangible output. Such farms would produce the type of crops or engage in the type of farming (livestock or cattle rearing) the zone is most favourable to support in line with the need of the nation.

The Ministry of Works constructs roads directly to all farm zones for both the private and public sector operators. Every week, the employees of each ministry are there in the hinterland to do the work while Abuja offices of the Ministry would have less than fifteen staff each. The job is not in Abuja but in the hinterland. The Minister of Power cannot sit in Abuja and know the situation of power supply to farms and manufacturers in the

villages across the zones. Government of professionals eradicates misplacement of priority and self-delusion in public office.

MINISTERIAL APPOINTMENT

In line with the principle of direct execution of projects by ministries, two categories of ministers are to be appointed. These are Task Ministers and Federal Ministers.

A) TASK MINISTERS: These are professionals to be appointed to head each ministry at the zonal or regional level. That is all Federal Ministries, excluding External Affairs, would have a Task Minister each as the arrow head throughout the six geo-political zones. Thus for Ministry of Education or Environment, there would be a Task Minister each in north East, North West, South West, South South, North Central and South East. Appointment of Task Ministers can be made by the President or the Federal Minister in charge of the ministry directly.

B) FEDERAL MINISTERS:

These are core members of the cabinet to be appointed by the Executive President as head of each Ministry at the Federal or National level. A Minister holds a National Portfolio and oversees activities in that regard throughout the Federation. By implication, six Task Ministers, one from each zone, report directly to the Federal Minister. With the approval of the President, a Federal Minister can fire a Task Minister especially on grounds of such acts as negligence, public misdemeanour, or misconduct or poor performance. Altogether, we would have 35 Federal Ministers throughout the Federation but 34 Task Ministers in each Zone (excluding External Affairs Ministry which does not exist in the Zone). In seeking nominees for the position of a Federal Minister, the President may consult with joint states executive forum of professions' associations or any such arms as he deems fit.

Appointment of Federal ministers must be subject of the National Assembly approval but not that of Task Ministers.

PRIMARY MINISTRIES

Due to the peculiar nature of their functions and absence of individual private sector operators directly linked to their portfolios,

certain ministries are better excluded from pack of legislative assembles. Such ministries include
- Internal Affairs
- Foreign Affairs
- Capital Territories and Local Government Affairs

The above listed would exist only as ministries of the Federal Government without corresponding Houses of profession or Constituency among the populace. However their functions and activities would be regulated by the National Assembly and General Assemblies as the case may be. For Foreign Affairs, former ambassadors and those trained in International Relation and Diplomacy may serve as the Constituents.

SECONDARY MINISTRIES

These are ministries with corresponding private sector publics or Houses in the geo-political zones. They include Agriculture and Raw Materials Ministry, Aviation, Commerce, Communication, Education, Engineering Technology, Environment, Finance, Food and Nutritional Substances, Health, Information, Industries, Justice, Labour and Productivity, Land and Housing, Petroleum and Allied Products, Police Affairs and Civil Security, Power and Steel, Science, Social Development, Solid Minerals, Sports, Tourism and Culture, Transport (Land), Transport (Sea), Water Resources, and Works Ministry.

MINISTRIES COLLECTIVE INTERDEPENDENCY
A re-organisation of Nigerian Ministries along this latitude of productivity and pragmatism would necessarily engender transformation. Transformation in perception, attitude and reaction, powered by new sense of belonging and freedom of expression. A professional who enjoys liberty to express his talent in his chosen field is naturally self-motivated. He experiences a sense of fulfill-

ment when that talent is turned into the product or service that can be measured, quantified acknowledged and put into use.

The New Nigeria vision enamours the ministries not only to employ distinguished professionals but also practically transform their talents into tangible results sustainably without going through intermediaries called contractors. Attraction and retention of egg heads, and resourceful deployment of their talents into tangible results are fulcrum of the secrets of so-called developed countries being celebrated today. The New Nigeria Vision is much potent and resourceful than what the developed nations of the West had ever achieved.

This vision provides a comprehensive solution package to the myriad of socio-political challenges of Nigeria, (the old Nigeria.)

By engendering a systematic approach to meeting needs, it fosters a consistent interdependence of ministries by awakening their consciousness to responsibility. Ministry of Rural and Urban Development for instance as one of the primary ministries, would map out each region or zone. This mapping provides the framework upon which other ministries would work. It draws out the master plan for residential, commercial areas; farming area, Industrial, Waste Collection points, Waste Treatment plants, Infrastructures - like Roads, Water reservoirs, Fire points, Government offices, Schools, Motor Parks, Major Markets, Manufacturers Channels, Industrial Estates (major, minor), etc. This interdependence of Federal Ministries would be made more pronounced by the salient principles of professionalism in that each Ministry is by implication compelled to do its own work fast so as not to delay the other ministries. For example, Works Ministry would have to construct Classroom blocks for Education, Roads for Agriculture and Transport etc.

CHAPTER 10

*The New Nigeria Does Not
Need a State Governor*

Between 1914 and 1960, a period of 45years, Nigeria had little or no inter-ethnic clashes under the administration of Britain. The year 1914 marked the amalgamation of its Northern and Southern Protectorates. However, from 1960 to 2005, another 45years with Nigerians administering Nigeria, ethnic-based social unrests have rocked all segments of the nation. A civil war of three years recorded massive killings and horrible experiences on both sides. Between 1985 and 2005 alone intra and inter-ethnic confrontations were recorded in North East, South East, North Central, South West and the South South regions of Nigeria. Obviously, both military and political party-based civil governments had been unable to free the country from ethnic consciousness and debacle. They lacked the foundation, character and appeal. Any government or position founded or occupied on the principle of ethnic bias within a nation, cannot in essence, contain or eradicate this albatross (ethnicity) instead, it would promote it consciously or unconsciously. In Nigeria, composition of State governments in all regions often brings about heightened ethnocentric chauvinism. Each ethnic group divides further into smaller unites whenever a state governor or commissioner is to be elected or selected. The society is plunged into unending definition and re-definition of filial ties. By so doing, governors and state functionaries merely see themselves as standing in for an ethnic group within a larger one. Unfortunately for the system and its people, ethnicity does not have an end. It expands and contracts with the imagination of its advocate.

One danger of ethnicity is that it gives ample room for those elected on its platform to divert state resources for personal aggrandizement. Whenever agitation arises from the people, public office holders, merely appease certain clans or families with palliative thus plunging the society into factions.
In itself, ethnic consciousness is antithetical to the spirit of nationhood and universal appeal and purpose of mankind. No country is made up of a singular family. Yet all nations or countries are from one source or descent. By shifting focus to universal appeal through needs, Libertocracy diverts attention from "what divides us" to "what unites us" as persons or a nation. Under Libertocracy therefore state governorship position is not needed.

A state governor would constitute a setback to the advancement of patriotism and sense of commitment to nationhood. State governorship splits the headship of government or body and dualises identity for the component units (individuals). Nationhood speaks of a singular identity. Once identity is allowed to be corporately and simultaneously dualised, it will give room for multiple allegiances. Loyalty will be impaired and infidelity would hold sway. Under such a circumstance, nation building becomes impossible because of fragmentation of will-power. In a nation yet to integrate its ethnic nationalities, multiple identities would give way to multiple pursuits and direction.

For an ethnically heterogeneous society like Nigeria, national planning and development would be better coordinated and enhanced without state governors. First, there will be room for sufficient harmonisation of the essence of federal ministers and the needs of the populace across the country. This harmony results from the removal of state governorship positions in the scheme of things. For instance, Nigeria has minister (s) for agriculture, water resources, aviation, communication, education, power and steel, information, and so on as cover one area of need or the other. What particular need of the people does a state governor represent? Since the Ministers are to function by providing these needs for the people who also live within each state of the federation, it amounts to unnecessary duplication of authority when state governors have to exercise supreme powers again over the people. By this, the ministers are naturally insulated from reaching the people. They do not have specific audience to assess them or ascertain their relevance to the system because, each state governor "shields" the people from the federal touch in the guise of asserting influence and authority.

Conversely, a nationally-focused government which influence and functions permeate all areas of need, is no doubt, better positioned to access the people and to be easily assessed uniformly by all sections of the nation. Sectarianism or ethnic bias would not be encouraged. Such a system for instance, would not have room for deferential treatment of "areas dominated by blacks" or "states populated by whites". Libertocracy represents people's needs and governs abilities through people. Without state governors and state governments, socio-economic development would be faster at regional and local levels. The presence of governors with far reaching powers (as it is), connotes two heads in a body. It hitches decision-flow process; notorious for breeding extraneous values. One head is the most appropriate design and fixture for the body. Delegation of powers from the federal to other unites such as regional and local levels, helps decisions at the topmost level to flow easily to all areas of the body or system. To have state government or governors with powers to make laws and direct the people otherwise is unhealthy and counter-productive.

For Nigeria, absence of state governments would eradicate double taxation, multiple statutory requirements, friction, double standard, and uncertainty in decision-making process. It would give room for coordinated policy direction at all levels and stimulate creativity.

Minister and indeed the Federal Government would be better tasked and challenged to become more sensitive and responsive to the people.

State governments, in Nigeria, breed corruption. Poor accountability and lack of standards are twin characteristics of state public service in Nigeria. Monthly, huge sums of money are shared to states from the federation account. There is no accountability or independent auditing of how these funds are spent by state governors. Again, via various unpopular devices, a number of state governments in Nigeria have increased tremendously their internally generated revenue into tens of billions of naira monthly. Citizens are milked and skinned through questionable taxes, yet public infrastructure are poorly managed and in many cases, non-existent. As if not enough, foreign nations had indicted and/or arrested some serving Nigerian state governors for money laundering offences. At the federal level in Nigeria, as at today, exists two instruments for fighting corruption. These are the Economic and Financial Crime Commission (EFCC) and the Independent Corrupt Practices Commission (ICPC). Through strident efforts, these two organs had recovered billions of naira from corrupt government officials. As ravaging as corruption has been to Nigeria, no state governor is bold enough to launch a campaign against corruption at their level.

With federal Ministries becoming visible and effective at the regional and by implication, the state levels, more income will be available for the development of the nation. Income to the federation account will soar up and the people will be better for it. Britain ruled Nigeria without appointing British officers as state governors. Yet, ethnic groups did not clash or fight themselves during British administration of the land, instead, the people collaborated (around their common needs) and forged a common front against oppression and colonialism. Today, our common problems are acts of godlessness manifesting in ethnicity, tribalism, individualism, mismanagement and corruption.

We will fare better to overcome all these without state governors and government.

CHAPTER 11

Capital Territories and Local Government Ministries

As the name implies, this ministry would focus mainly on two major functions. These are:
a. Maintenance of federal capital territories and
b. Coordination of local government affairs throughout the federation.

ZONAL CAPITAL TERRITORIES
Abuja should become the Central Capital Territory, and in addition, Vision of the New Nigeria wishes to recommend that each zone of SW, NE, NW, SE, NC and SS should have a capital to be known as zonal capital. This is primarily, to facilitate zonal coordination effort among decision makers; galvanise speedy responses or promptness and easy access to vital information, it is the combination of the Central and the Zonal Capitals that should make up the new Federal Capital Territories.

For ease of administration therefore, VNN posits that zonal capitals should be the middle points among the six or seven states that make up a region or zone.

CHAPTER 12

The Judiciary

In extending professionalism style of governance to the judiciary, certain cardinal principles have to be followed.

1. First, to ensure that justice is not delayed. This means that the court process(es) must be carried out with dispatch and accuracy.
2. The process of obtaining justice must not be expensive.
3. Judges and lawyers must not be over-loaded or overburdened at every point in time.
4. Every lawyer or advocate must be able to assist the state to dispense justice accordingly so that an offender gets appropriate punishment or sanction while an oppressed person is not left to suffer but duly compensated.
5. By implication therefore, the role of Lawyers (like Insurance Brokers or Stockbrokers) has to be properly re-defined. A lawyer should not profit by shielding an offender from punishment or aiding evasion of compensation or freedom to the oppressed.

A) THE COURT SYSTEM

In the New Nigeria, let the court be categorised or allowed to function according to the area of needs of the populace. To this end, there should be specific courts along the underlisted lines.

(1) Corporate Affairs Courts: to cover or handle issues on:
- Company Registration Matters
- Board membership and regulation
- Buy-over modalities. Stamp Duties etc.
- Shares allotment
- Annual report Publications, requirements and conditions
-Stock Trading Matters relating to shares ownership
- Dividend sharing, including transfer and inheritance
- Limit of ownership
- Trusteeship etc.

(2) Environmental Court:
- Air pollution
- Illegal conversion of buildings
- Sewage Disposal
- Waste Disposal
- Noise Pollution
- Effluents
- Illegal Citing etc.

(3) State Revenue Courts

. Tax Matters
. Toll fees
. Business Premises fees
. Any evasion of state charges/Tax
. Import Duty - underpayment etc
. Connivance with public officials

(4) Financial Practice and Commerce
- Banking

- Mortgage
- Insurance
- Stock Brokers
- Accounting firms
- Importation of banned goods
- Professionality Issues including membership of Institutes
- Finance Houses
- Forex Operations etc
- Illegal Trading

(5) Health and Pharmaceutical Matters
- All matters thereon

(6) Metroplis Court
- Traffic law violation
- Prostitution
- Drunkenness
- Unapproved Blockade of Streets
- Smoking in Public places etc.

(7) Internal Affairs Court
- Passport issuance
- Permit for foreigners
- False Identity or Impersonation
- Visa Racketeering
- Forgery of government or public document or private sector document.
- Prison mismanagement et al

(8) Education Court

- Exam malpractices
- Fake Results

- Sale or Peddling of fake Exam Questions
- Occultism in campuses
- Sexual harassment in campuses etc.

(9) Public Asset Court

. Stealing or Pilfering Government or Public Asset
. Vandalisation of Public Property
. Betrayal of Public Trust
. Connivance to make Government lose Revenue etc
. Mismanagement
. Illegal mining

(10) Marriage Affairs Court

(11) State Affairs Court

. Issues concerning cardinal principles of nationhood e.g Discrimination arising from state of origin as against the new federal principle of place of residence
. State security matters
. Nepotism
. Ethnic nationalism or championing

(12) General Matters

- Human Rights etc

(13) Constitutional Court/Jurisprudence

(14) Copyright and Inventions

(15) Rent and Property
(16) Labour
(17) Agriculture and Export

(18) Special Courts
. Robbery
. Illegal Possession of arms
. Membership of ethnic militia
. Unauthorised Arrest and Detention
. Kidnapping
. Ritual Killings

B). PROFESSIONALISING LAW CHAMBERS

Now, this streamlining of courts and specialisation would also set the stage for lawyers. Legal practitioners would choose two areas of interest to work. For example, a lawyer may choose to be registered with Agriculture and Export and copyright matters. Such a lawyer cannot handle any matter outside of those two or three as the case may be.

However there could be exemptions for lawyers (as individuals) who had become Senior Advocate of Nigeria for say 10 years and above.

C). GROUPING OF JUDICIAL COURTS

The specialisation of courts as highlighted above can be re-grouped into seven main types. These are:

i. Economic Sabotage Matters Chambers: Those concentrating on

Corporate Affairs Commission issues like company registration, representation, shares allotment and ownership matters. State revenue matters, Financial practice and Commerce, Public asset, Financial fraud, Tax matters.

ii. Public Interest Matters Chambers
Offence under metropolis such as traffic offences, noise pollution, illegal closure and occupation of streets etc. Issues under Internal affairs, State Affairs Matters.

iii. Healthcare Matters
Hospital management, Drugs importation and sales, fake drugs, Patent matters, Drug manufacturing & specification. Medical professionals misconduct, Environmental hazards.

iv. Matters of Personal Interest
Educational issues, Copyright and invention, Labour, Rent and property, Religion etc, Human rights.

v. Constitutional Interest Matters
Issues on limitations of arms or organs of government, Electioneering matters, Membership of a Profession, External affairs, Appointments into local or foreign offices, Membership of foreign or international organization.

vi. Special Interest Matters
Special courts, Export matters, Marriage, Agriculture.

vii. Others.

Each of these courts should be available in the six zones of North West, North East, North Central, South South, South East and

South West. Zonal Headquarters could serve as Appellate court for lower courts of same jurisdiction or the six zones may have three super-ordinate courts (as may be deemed fit) before referring to the Supreme Court. No case before a court should go beyond two weeks (hearing and ruling) and all appeals to the Supreme Court level to be sorted out within three weeks.

D.) AMMENDMENT TO COURT PROCEEDINGS

(a) This should be re-appraised and revolutionized to reveal truth and enthrone justice in the real sense of it. For example: An accused person or his lawyer should be asked in a court session:

- Did you or she/he commit the offence or not? OR
- Which of these things did you (he/she) do or actually commit? And no longer the usual question of:
Are you guilty or not? because the latter gives room for evasion of facts and truth.

(b) PRELIMINARY TECHNICALITIES

(i) The court Registry should be reinvigorated. Registrars should, at the point of filing a case, examine and ascertain the court's jurisdiction to handle the case. If the court is not competent to handle the case, the registrar should immediately refer it to the court of competent jurisdiction.

(ii) After the case is registered, a proof of certainty must be stamped or effected. By this, no case would allow for argument on jurisdiction but if the Registrar fails to do his work properly, then he/she or they would be suspended or penalized appropriately.

(iii) All court proceedings should be computerized including identification and registration of lawyers, their chambers and judgements. Evidence should be properly documented including pictures/photographs of accused persons or criminals.

E) GENERAL RE-ORIENTATION

The law and lawyers should operate in a way to show that their essence is to ensure that an offender is punished (not to be freed or made to jump penalty). Also that the just or oppressed is duly compensated or relieved from oppression. Anything contrary to these is itself against the principle of justice. A system that allows Lawyers to feed fat on shielding offenders from penalty is a promoter of injustice.

Lawyers can argue for a reduction in penalty or punishment (depending on the provisions of the law) But not to engage in frivolities or other issues aimed at diverting attention from the real matter at stake. Every lawyer should know whether or not his client

commits the offence before appearing. Any misrepresentation by the lawyer that is discovered later (with evidence) should attract a heavy penalty against the lawyer including fine, suspension or label of "Non-suitable professional".

CHAPTER 13

Citizenship

The Vision of the New Nigeria provides for a re-definition of citizenship of the country. A new name, a new orientation, a new method or approach to governance. A shift from the mentality of old because the union and identity are no longer based on the usual ethnic background or biological history. The citizenship of the New Nigeria is therefore defined on the basis of where a person lives and makes his daily contribution in terms of human endeavour. The wisdom behind this citizenship is that each person is reckoned with on the basis of meaningful contribution he/she makes toward meeting the need of others wherever they live within the nation.

If you live in Kano may be for five years and do engage in sales of yam or tomato in Kano, you are simply a citizen of Nigeria in Kano whether your name is EMEKA NNAJI or YUSUF USMAN, your state is simply kano. And you can no longer be registered in any other State or Local government except you are delisted from the former (on transfer or relocation). Name or state of origin are no longer the relevant things in the New Nigeria as far as identification is concerned. It is simply unwise to have somebody living in Port Harcourt all through the year but could only be reckoned with as a citizen of Kebbi State simply because his parents hailed from Kebbi. Such practices are outdated in this Vision of the New

Nigeria. We can ask the question(s):

What tribe does God like within Nigeria! Which ethnic group does God hate in Nigeria? Which ethnic group is God Himself? What language does God speak? Is it Hausa, Ibo, Yoruba or Efik?

God did not not make anyone Ibo or Hausa or Yoruba before birth. A child can only cry out at birth, cannot speak Ibo or Hausa, or Yoruba or any tribal language. It is what we teach the child after birth he or she would grow up with. So, the New Nigeria is not suitable for tribalists or ethnocentrists who hate others simply because of the language they speak. God hates evil, - deceit, fornication, adultery, stealing, lying tongues, greed, embezzlement of public fund, idol worshipping, selfishness - and not language.

By implication therefore, the New Nigeria provides that a citizen of Kebbi - whatever be his/her name - has equal rights with all other citizens of Kebbi. Any segregation or ill treatment meted out to him becomes an offence against the nation.

In the same manner, an Emeka Kalu who is based in Jigawa and therefore a citizen of Jigawa state, must contribute his quota there. The right hand washes the left and so does the left to the right and the two will be better for it.
The New Nigeria citizenry is one which produces a Yusuf Zakariyau representing Imo state, an Akin Akindele representing Sokoto State, Dofan Gboko from Cross River

State, Onyebuchi Ononye representing Kano state, Bala Malumfachi representing Osun staten Kokori Igbrude from Kwara State. It reckons directly with talents, God's gifting and endowment as manifestation of divine grace for solving collective problems or difficulties. It recognises that God's way of distributing these resources is borne out of superior wisdom, which is above and beyond the ability of man. The need of one man is encapsulated in the gift of the other and vice versa. This platform of re-defined citizenship guarantees freedom to live, excel and engage in healthy competitive cooperation. There is so much deposited in us by God our Creator, let us help ourselves, through harmonious living, to "exhume" for a more beneficial use, part of this resourceful endowment.

CHAPTER 14

The Local Government System

L IBERTOCRACY provides for a local government adminis-tration that reflects a true grassroots system of govern-ance.

A grassroots system of governance cannot afford to be distant from the people at the lowest wrung of the ladder and this is aptly captured by this Vision.

Whether by practice or orientation, a true grassroots system is one which makes the government un-detachable from the people it governs on day in day out basis. This is clearly expressed under the following headings.

(A) STRATEGIC LAYOUT
The number of housing units in each local government area should be determined with high level of accuracy. Street by street, every portion of each local government area must be spelt out or properly documented in the local government Long Book and Computers. House, tents or structure in each local government must be numbered and or properly identified in the Long Book and Computer Systems including ownership of the houses or property,

structure or type. Having known the streets, they should then be grouped into Districts depending on population density or number of housing units. The Districts can be named A, B, C, D, E, or 1, 2, 3, 4, 5, 6 etc to make up the number of Districts per local government area.

(B) UNDERLYING PRINCIPLE

i. First, in line with the national principles for citizenship an individual or Nigerian is a citizen of where he/she lives or is settled for the purpose of making his/her living. Place of origin does not exist in the citizenship portfolio of the New Nigeria and so it is with the local government.

ii. Upon assumption of office, all elected officials automatically become representatives of the local government and no longer that of their place or districts within the local government.

iii. Each representative would function universally in a portfolio. That is he or she is representing the people's need and not an ethnic group.

iv. The local government administration would not give out contracts to anyone for the construction of roads, or public utilities instead, it would directly execute projects including provision of portable water, roads, schools, hospitals and medical facilities, revenue generation etc

v. Official Language of communication in every government office is English, so no one can be discriminated against on the basis of tongue. Interpretation to those who do not understand English is secondary and should not be stretched beyond its limit.

vi. No one person can belong to two local governments or Districts at the same time. Your particulars must be erased in one for the individual to belong to another.

ELECTION INTO LOCAL GOVERNMENT POSITIONS

Each District within the local government area to elect 20 or 24 people as their representatives on non party basis. No political party and so candidates for election may be selected or raised through Residents Associations among the districts.

Each District's Resident Association would elect its own executives for the association that would co-ordinate activities at that level particularly concerning primary elections and feedback programmes.

If the constitution for instance allows a maximum of 12 Districts per local government area (a local government may decide to have less.) Then each District, through the Residents Associations, would elect or produce two candidates to represent it. Thus, each local government would have 24 elected representatives. These 24 in turn, would be split into two equal groups of 12 each, to be called the Shadow Group & the Select Group.

(A) THE SHADOW GROUP

Each candidate with the highest number of votes at the District primary election becomes a Shadow Representative. In other words, out of the two candidates elected by the District, the one who pulls (polls) the highest vote count will not be made a councillor but a shadow representative of the local government. These shadow Reps would be 12 in number indicating one person per district.

POWER AND FUNCTIONS OF THE SHADOW GROUP

1. To monitor the select group (Councillors) and report their activ-

ities to the District Association and electorate regularly.

2. To guide against misplacement of priority by the councillors.

3. Ensure active mobilization of the local government populace for direct execution of laudable project more so that such projects (like provision of water, roads or rural electrification or gutter construction and all infrastructural facilities) would no longer be awarded to any contractor but directly handled by employees (both full and short-term employees).

The Shadow Group would be fully remunerated by the local government and each to be on the same salary scale with the councillors.

The difference in their monthly package would be in area of allowances for example while the councillor would be entitled to housing allowance the shadow Rep. would not but each would have official vehicle.

POWER OF THE SHADOW GROUP

Should be empowered to impeach any councillor who is found to be incapable or whose performance is rated below average. The group should have the power to summon or request information from the councillor whenever the group needs such. Two third majority votes of the Shadow Reps. should be able to unseat a councillor.

SHADOW GROUP LIMITATIONS

1. A Shadow Rep can not replace a councillor under any reason only the Districts or electorate can vote for a new councillor in case of any impeachment.

2. A Shadow Rep cannot act for the councillor in absence or when the latter is on vacation or official leave or assignment.

3. Shadow group cannot impeach the chairman of the local government only the councillors can do or the electorates of all the 12

Districts.

(B) THE SELECT GROUP
This is the group that forms the government of the local government directly. Its members are councillors and 12 in number. These councillors are those who score next to the Shadow Rep in the election at the District level. To be a councillor, you must not be the overall winner of the election at your district but must score at least 45% (forty-five percent) of the total vote cast in the District. If the vote count is less than 45% another election should be conducted for the overall winner and a new candidate.

FUNCTIONALITY & RELEVANCE OF THE SELECT GROUP

Each councillor like the Shadow Representative is to represent the whole local government. By this therefore, the councillor is to function according to the need of the local government not the interest of his/her own District. Thus we would have councillor to handle portfolios or areas of needs as Educational Administration, Street Cleaning or Environment, Water Distribution or Resources, Commerce, Housing and Rent, Works, Social Development & Recreation, Agriculture, Health etc.

Each councillor would therefore have a portfolio in the light of an identified area of need and develop a universal programme of action for District 1, 2, 3, to 12. He or she is no longer to concentrate on his own primary district or where he lives. So, the Shadow Rep would also function along this area of the portfolio. Whatever programme Works Councillor develops for District 1 or 2 must also get to District 12. Exemptions can only be allowed for emergencies

ELECTION OF LOCAL GOVERNMENT CHAIRMAN (NORMAL)

Among the 12 councillors representing each District, the three with the highest vote counts as councillors should be selected for scrutiny by a body to be known as D-12. This D-12 should be made of the chairmen or delegates of the Principal Resident Association of each district (or District Associations). The purpose of the scrutiny is to vet certificates and other claims of these councillors and possibly allow for the public to double-check them for any criminal record.

Among these three, the councillor whose vote is in-between the first and the last should be picked as the chairman of the Local Government. When there is a tally in their votes, the third person, that is the person with the lowest vote count should become the chairman.

TENURE OF OFFICE FOR LOCAL GOVERNMENT

For councillors, chairman of local government and shadow group, the tenure is the same. While councillors can run two or three terms maximum, the Shadow Group should have no limit. As long as the electorate wishes to re-elect a Shadow Rep, no constitutional restraint should prevent it.

QUALIFICATIONS INTO LOCAL GOVERNMENT ELECTION

For the position of councilor, Chairman or Shadow Rep, a candidate must have a minimum of Ordinary National Diploma (OND) or substitute in terms of experience say ten years of working in a reputable organization at managerial position.

REMOVAL OF LOCAL GOVERNMENT OFFICIALS

District representatives or delegates can withdraw or discharge a Shadow Rep if he/she is found to be incompetent or of poor performance. Same way an incompetent councillor can be removed by his/her District Association if two-third of the members vote accordingly. Two-third votes of the shadow group should also be able to remove a councillor should he/she be found wanting especially for principal offences e.g failure to appear before the Shadow Group, poor record of accountability, consistent negligence or failure to attend Grassroots Day, two times consecutively etc

The councillors via a two-third or Majority vote can remove or impeach the chairman of the Local Government but cannot elect another one. However, one of the councillors can be mandated to act as chairman pending election of a new chairman. The Joint District Associations (of all the 10 or 12 Districts) can remove a serving chairman or councillors and elect new one by two-third majority.

CHAPTER 15

Grassroots Day

Mandatorily, a day (Saturday or Sunday) should be set aside as Grassroots Day once in three or four weeks. The Local Government Chairman must address representatives of each street or District and the public on all issues concerning the Local Government. Venue for this forum must be an open place within the Local Govt area and can be shifted from District to District (every month or quarter). Issues to be discussed would include (but not limited to)

a) Finances - Income and Expenditure profile
b) Projects for the next month
c) Welfarist Programmes including old people homes, orphanage, motherless babies, widowhood.
d) Health etcetera.

Councillors and lieutenants of the chairman may also be mandated at the forum to answer questions from the people. Voting on any issue at the Grassroots Day on any subject or project must be taken seriously. The Shadow Group must participate actively in the Grassroots Day and provide useful information to the public. Every Local Government must submit evidence of its Grassroots

Day to the Federal office of Local Government Affairs and Capital Territories Ministry on monthly basis. Failure to do so automatically disqualifies the local government from Federation Account allocation for the next month (s) and in addition to other disciplinary measures the Federal Government may decide to take.

This federal office must also vet regularly the information contained in video recording and other materials submitted to it by the local government. Grey areas or issues not satisfactorily treated by the local government chairman during the Grassroots Forum should be revisited and ironed out.

SONGS OF THE NEW NIGERIA
(Libertocracy)

CHORUS:
No, no, no, no
No hurting
No, no, no, no
No dissension

1) Coming together in the mountain of the Lord
Dwelling together by the power of His love
The wolves and the lamb in the mountain of the Lord
Singing, no hurting.
Chorus: No, no, no etc

2) Ibo-Yoruba in the New Nigeria
No more hatred among Hausa-Fulani
Dwelling together in the New Nigeria, without dissension.
Chorus: No, no, no etc

3) Ijaw-Hausa in warm embrace forever
Urhobo-Fulani living together in oneness
Tsekhiri and Ijaw in the power of God's love,
Singing no hurting
Chorus: No, no, no etc

4) Kebbi Yobe, Osun Abia, Bayelsa
Niger Bauchi, Lagos Rivers, Enugu
Delta, Kano in the New Nigeria
Singing no hurting
Chorus: No, no, no etc

5) Sokoto, Taraba, Oyo, Imo, & Edo
Gombe, Kogi, Zamfara, Ekiti
Ebonyi, Ogun, Plateau Akwa-Ibom
Singing no hurting.
Chorus: No, no, no etc

6) Adamawa, Katsina Cross-Rivers,
Kwara Ondo, Anambra, Kaduna
Nasarawa, in the New Nigeria
Singing no hurting.
Chorus: No, no, no etc

7) Coming together in the mountain of the Lord
Dwelling together in the power of His love
Jigawa, Borno living together with Benue
Singing no hurting.
Chorus: No, no, no etc

8) People of God, you are New Nigerians
No more prejudice against tribe or language
Idoma, Efik make no difference in our lives
Because no hurting.

Chorus: No, no, no, no
    No hurting
        No, no, no, no
        No dissension

ABOUT THE BOOK

Ordinarily, defining "democracy as the government of the people, by the people and for the people" looks harmless, inspiring and promising. In practice however, democracy has not been the government of the people and by the people.

Involvement of political party system in constituting government disallows people from owning it. It is the government of the ruling political party (or parties) and not the people.

Party system is a political veil, an ideological gimmick separating the people from a government that ought to be theirs. Whether it is called Labour Party, Conservative, Social Democratic, Republican (or Grand Old Party), Peoples Democratic Party or All Progressive Congress, it does not represent any area of need of the society and so it is irrelevant in any nation.

Political parties are leeches on the spirit of democracy. They hijack the institution of government and usurp the position of the people. Nigeria is terminally handicapped by political party system just as humanity is denied the benefits derivable from representative government.

Party system is a cankerworm to the stem of Democratic practice. It prices democracy above the reach and affordability of the majority of the people in a nation. It reserves its platforms for the super - rich, party henchmen and privileged individuals. Parties breed and corrupt politicians who in turn corrupt the civil servants, electoral umpires and the judiciary.

How to eradicate corruption in politics, attract widespread and qualitative participation in governance and make government belong to the people in word and action; in orientation, principle and manifestation are contained in Libertocracy : Vision of the New Nigeria.

With LIBERTOCRACY, ethnic groups within a nation can be easily integrated; nationalities across countries unified and races across the globe desegregated. It is the panacea for continental, subregional and confederations like European Union, African Union and United Nations.

ACKNOWLEDGEMENT

Glory to God in the highest for all aspects of this work. It is a manifestation of His awesome grace and an attestation to the timeless truth that His name is near.

My foremost appreciation to my parents for their invaluable contributions to educate, and more importantly, instill discipline and the Fear of God in me. I want to thank God also for the teachers I had passed through in acquiring primary, post primary and university education. Also to friends, relations and all those who, consciously and unconsciously, had imparted to me the real substance of life in the course of my growing up, I say bravo.

Men raised or dedicated by God to support the putting together of this book deserve much commendation. In this regard, I acknowledge the remarkable contributions of people like, Bro Wole Olakunle, untiring supporters like Messrs Olusola Adebiyi, Kolawole Olujimi and Samuel Bamigboye. Also, I owe some gratitude to Mr Rotimi Sodipo and Sola Ogunsola, who assisted me while composing the songs of the New Nigeria, the Songs of liberty, unification and integration.

Very special thanks to Mr Mudashiru Atanda Adeniyi and Mrs Aduke Adeniyi for their hospitality. For their care, love and kindness, I wish to appreciate Mr and Mrs Abayomi (Scorol) Akindusoye, Mr Ayo Obideyi, Solomon Alalade among others.

To the under listed, I dare to say thank you for your endurance, understanding and cooperation - Heritage, Zadok and Ezekiel Obideyi. May God strengthen and uphold you in the power of His might.

ABOUT THE AUTHOR

Yemi Obideyi

YEMI OBIDEYI trained as a sociologist between 1987 and 1991 in Ondo State University, Ado - Ekiti (now Ekiti State), South Western part of Nigeria. For a number of years, he worked with the Daily Times of Nigeria PLC, as a journalist reporting news and events for Business Times, a subsidiary publication of the Daily Times group. In 1999, he joined Global Bank PLC, a commercial banking institution in Lagos, Nigeria, where he functioned variously as officer and later Head of the banks Corporate Affairs unit. He was saddled with handling the banks reputation management. In mainstream banking, he had a stint in Treasury Operation, Interbank Trading, Account Management and marketing. Obideyi also worked in plastics manufacturing company as a manager and later director of Logistics.

BOOKS BY THIS AUTHOR

Libertocracy - Re-Inventing Democracy

www.ingramcontent.com/pod-product-compliance
Lightning Source LLC
Chambersburg PA
CBHW061358250726
48657CB00004B/1555